Journey Through The BIBLE

The Rev. Dr. Rebecca Abts Wright, the writer of this study book, is Associate Professor of Old Testament at The School of Theology, The University of the South, Sewanee, Tennessee. Dr. Wright is a clergy member of the Baltimore-Washington Annual Conference of The United Methodist Church and has pastored churches in West Virginia, Maryland, and Connecticut. She has also taught, mostly in the area of Old Testament subjects, at Wesley Theological Seminary and at Yale Divinity School. Dr. Wright's family includes two daughters (Helen Kate and Anna Miriam), a dog, and a cat.

JOURNEY THROUGH THE BIBLE: EXODUS, LEVITICUS, NUMBERS, DEUTERONOMY. An official resource for The United Methodist Church prepared by the General Board of Discipleship through the division of Church School Publications and published by Cokesbury, a division of The United Methodist Publishing House; 201 Eighth Avenue, South; P.O. Box 801; Nashville, TN 37202. Printed in the United States of America. Copyright © 1994 by Cokesbury. All rights reserved.

To order copies of this publication, call toll free 800-672-1789. Call Monday—Friday 7:30—5:00 Central Time or 8:30—4:30 Pacific Time. Use your Cokesbury account, American Express, Visa, Discover, or MasterCard.

10 11 12 13 14 — 19 18 17 16

EDITORIAL TEAM
Donn Downall,
Editor
Norma L. Bates,
Assistant Editor
Linda O. Spicer,
Adult Section
Assistant

DESIGN TEAM
Susan J. Scruggs,
Design Supervisor,
Cover Design
Teresa B. Travelstead,
Designer

ADMINISTRATIVE STAFF
Neil M. Alexander,
Vice-President,
Publishing
Duane A. Ewers,
Editor of Church
School Publications
Gary L. Ball-Kilbourne,
Executive Editor of
Adult Publications

Cokesbury

╭ABLE OF CONTENTS

Volume 2: Exodus—Deuteronomy   by Rebecca Abts Wright

Art and Photo Credits: pp. 10, 101, 108, 109, Ron Hester; pp. 15, 48, © 1987 Biblical Archaeological Society; p. 17, © 1981 Biblical Archaeological Society; pp. 58, 77, © Cleo Freelance Photo; p. 90, Charles Cox.

$\mathcal{J}$NTRODUCTION TO THE SERIES

Welcome to JOURNEY THROUGH THE BIBLE!
You are about to embark on an adventure that can change your life.

WHAT TO BRING WITH YOU

Don't worry about packing much for your trip. All you need to bring with you on this journey are
- an openness to God speaking to you in the words of Scripture
- companions to join you on the way, and
- your Bible

ITINERARY

In each session of this volume of JOURNEY THROUGH THE BIBLE, first you will be offered some hints for what to look for as you read the Bible text, and then you will be guided through four "dimensions" of study. Each is intended to help you through a well-rounded appreciation and application of the Bible's words.

HOW TO PREPARE FOR YOUR JOURNEY THROUGH THE BIBLE

Although you will gain much if all you do is show up for Bible study and participate willingly in the session, you can do a few things to gain even more.
- Read in advance the Bible passage mentioned in What to Watch For, using the summaries and hints as you read.
- During your Bible reading, answer the questions in Dimension 1.
- Read the rest of the session in this study book.
- Try a daily discipline of reading the Bible passages suggested in Dimension 4. Note that the Bible texts listed in Dimension 4 do *not* relate to a particular session. But if you continue with this daily discipline, by the end of thirteen weeks, you will have read through *all* of that portion of the Bible covered by this volume.

Studying the Bible is a lifelong project. JOURNEY THROUGH THE BIBLE provides you with a guided tour for a few of the steps along your way. May God be with you on your journey!

Gary L. Ball-Kilbourne
Executive Editor, Adult Publications
Church School Publications

Questions or comments?
Call Curric-U-Phone 1-800-251-8591.

$\mathcal{S}$ETTING THE SCENE

What to Watch For

We call this second book of the Bible "Exodus." The word, according to the dictionary, refers to the departure of a large number of people. The name signifies the great liberating act of God on behalf of Israel. The Hebrew way of naming biblical books, however, is to use the first significant word as the title. In this case it is *names*; and the book is known in Hebrew as *Shemot*, or (the English translation) *Names*. Note how often in these first two chapters of Exodus we know, or do not know, the names of the characters.

For this chapter read Exodus 1:1–2:25. In many cases names of "important" persons will not be mentioned; but names of some seemingly "insignificant" characters will be given. Along with names, and thus identity, "knowing" will play a large role in Exodus. We will find a pharaoh who does not "know" Joseph. From that ignorance will flow fear, which leads to oppression and suffering. The sister and the mother of baby Moses will be among those who are "in the know." We will see that neither the good guys, the bad guys, nor the powerful people necessarily belong to the groups we might expect.

3

1. Why is the pharaoh afraid? (Exodus 1:9-10)

2. What does he propose? (Exodus 1:11, 13-16)

3. Why don't his plans work? (Exodus 1:17)

4. Who has the most power in Exodus 1 and 2? Which characters are able to accomplish their own purposes?

Exodus 1:1-6 is a hinge between Genesis and Exodus, giving a brief reminder of why the Israelites are in Egypt. These verses assume familiarity with the content of Genesis 39–50 in which Jacob's family came initially as guests, even as honored guests. Verse 7 also refers back to God's blessing in Creation, noted at Genesis 1:28, with the repetition of three of the same verbs: "be fruitful," "multiply," and "fill the earth." Part of God's ancient promise to Abraham is thus coming to pass (Genesis 12:2; 15:5; 17:1-8), although it happens in a different place.

The change in the situation is signaled by 1:8: "Now a new king arose over Egypt, who did not know Joseph." Note two things. First, the ruler is never named. "Pharaoh" and "king" are both titles, not personal names. Second, the only piece of information we are given about him is that he "did not know Joseph." Why should that be his identification? How could he possibly be expected to know someone who is long since dead?

The verb translated here "know" (*yada*) will be significant throughout Exodus. It means more than the ability to recite a particular fact and can include notions of familiarity with, and intimacy with, including sexual intimacy between husband and wife. Comprehension and understanding as well as cognition are implied in the Hebrew word. When used in relational contexts, "it bespeaks a relationship of depth in which there is commitment to those who are known and genuine concern regarding their welfare" (From *Exodus: Interpretation: A Bible Commentary for Teaching and Preaching*, by Terence E. Fretheim; John Knox Press, 1991; page 27). This new king did not know about Joseph. He was not acquainted with the history of Joseph's family in Egypt. He knew neither the Israelites' story nor the famine and the deliverance that intertwined their history with his own.

> This new pharaoh did not know about Joseph. He was not acquainted with the history of Joseph's family in Egypt. He knew neither the Israelites' story nor the famine and the deliverance that intertwined their history with his own.

From this ignorance arises fear and the call to "deal shrewdly" with the Israelites. Even in stating the problem as he sees it, the king does not seem particularly "shrewd": he does not want the Israelites to keep increasing in number, but he also does not want them to leave (1:9-10).

His solutions are no less problematic. First comes the hard labor. But this does not work, for "the more they were oppressed, the more they multiplied and spread" (1:12a).

Plan number two involves midwives, Shiphrah and Puah, and the command that they kill the Hebrews' boy babies and allow the girls to live (1:15-21). Is this a shrewd plan? True, it would get rid of potential soldiers, but it would also reduce the number of slaves. And a population can grow faster with a surplus of women than with a surplus of men. Somehow Pharaoh discovers that the midwives are not carrying out his plan and he questions them. "Hebrew women are not like the Egyptian women," they tell him, turning his own faulty thinking back on itself.

> "She saw that he was a fine baby." "And God saw that it was good." Even in the midst of persecution and oppression, there are echoes of the goodness of God's Creation.

In desperation the king proclaims a third plan. "Then Pharaoh commanded all his people, 'Every boy that is born to the Hebrews you shall throw into the Nile' " (1:22). The phrase "to the Hebrews" does not appear in the Hebrew text, although it is in some ancient translations. Perhaps the phrase was indeed absent. Perhaps Pharaoh was so out-of-control, so powerless in his power, so foolish in his shrewd dealings, that he mistakenly gave a ridiculous command that *all* boy babies be thrown into the Nile.

Chapter 2 moves the focus from the universal command to one little family. A man and woman marry, the woman conceives and has a boy. Verse 2b says "she saw that he was a fine baby." We may see here another echo of the recurring phrase in Genesis 1: "and God saw that it was good."

5

Even in the midst of persecution and oppression, there are echoes of the goodness of God's creation.

After three months, the mother can no longer hide the baby at home, and she makes a "basket" for him. The actual word is *tebah* (tay-BAW) or ark, a word used in the Bible only here and in the story of Noah in Genesis 6–9. (The word used for the Ark of the Covenant later in the Old Testament is a different Hebrew word. Both mean "box.") Would the people hearing and reading this account in those early centuries have thought to themselves, "Oh, look. This word is used in only two stories in the whole Bible"? No, probably not. But they likely would have made a mental connection between Moses and Noah—and even with God's several acts of saving through water. It would be similar to a mother's saying to a son helping set the table for a festive meal, "Use the goblets," rather than "Use the chalices." A goblet and a chalice have the same shape and are made to hold liquids for drinking, but "chalice" carries religious overtones and connotations not present with "goblet." In this story, the use of the word ark (*tebah*) is a signal to the alert audience that something special is taking place.

The focus then turns to the familiar story of the baby's rescue by Pharaoh's daughter and the delightful irony of her hiring the baby's own mother to care for him. She names him "Moses," saying, "because I drew him out of the water." This is a folk tradition for the name—a later explanation built on similar-sounding words. If Pharaoh's daughter had been a better linguist, she might have recognized that the grammatical form of *Moses* could be translated "one who draws through [the water]" and thus be an even clearer hint of what is to come for all the Israelites through Moses.

What was Moses looking for as he turned one way and another? To see if he was being observed? Perhaps. Or maybe he was looking to see where the authorities were, looking for an overseer, or anyone in command, to whom he could report the infraction and thus not have to become further involved himself.

We know nothing else of Moses' childhood. In the next story he is an adult. Moses goes out one day "to his people" and sees "their forced labor." That is, he sees the situation as it is, as it is described in 1:11. He also sees an Egyptian "beating" a Hebrew, with the repeated note "one of his kinsfolk." Moses turns around and, seeing no one, kills the Egyptian. He then hides the body. Verse 12 can be read in several ways. What was Moses looking for as he turned one way and another? To see if he was being observed? Perhaps. Or maybe he was looking to see where the authorities were, looking for an overseer, or anyone in command, to whom he could report the infraction and thus not have to become further involved himself. The text is silent about motive. What also does not come through in translation is that

6

Moses struck once, when the Egyptian had been striking repeatedly. Did he not know his own strength, that a single blow became a fatal accident? Again, we are not told.

The next day Moses goes out and sees two Hebrews struggling. He tries to break up the fight and is taunted, "Do you mean to kill me as you did the Egyptian?" Realizing his secret is known, Moses flees.

Moses' concern for justice continues to play itself out in the midst of a comical episode. The priest of Midian had seven unmarried daughters! Other shepherds would wait until these girls had drawn water for their father's flock, then they would push in and let their own sheep drink first. Moses chases them away, and the girls are able to get home earlier than usual. Upon learning that a stranger ("an Egyptian") helped them, their father demands to know why they left him cooling his heels back at the well. "Bring him home to supper!" he orders. One thing leads to another; and in the narrator's compressed time scale of two verses, Moses and Zipporah marry and have a son, whom Moses names Gershom (2:21-22). This is a word-play on the Hebrew for "a sojourner [or alien] there" as a reminder that Moses is not at home.

The narrator next reports that the pharaoh who sought Moses' life has died and that the plight of the Israelites was not thereby relieved. They "cry out." The text does not say they cry specifically to God, but that their cry "rose up." God heard it.

With 2:24, God returns as a character in the story. The four verbs in the final two verses are highly significant, as is the unusual fourfold repetition of the subject noun: God heard, God remembered, God looked upon, and God took notice. There is no object for the verb "took notice" in the Hebrew, though most English translations supply one.

Many themes of Exodus, and indeed of the whole Bible, are introduced in these two chapters. A lack of knowledge of one's history, community, or self leads to disaster. There are contrasts made with the relish of irony between wisdom and foolishness and between power and weakness. In

FIVE FEMALES WHO THWART PHARAOH'S PLANS

Shiphrah, midwife (Exodus 1:15)
Puah, midwife, (Exodus 1:15)
Jochebed, Moses' mother (Exodus 2:1-2, 9b-10a; 6:20)
Miriam, Moses' sister (Exodus 2:4, 7; 15:20)
Pharaoh's daughter (Exodus 2:5-6, 10)

these two chapters, five females, by doing normal and ordinary and expected things, frustrate the king's plans. Was he not afraid of them because he did not think mere women could do anything important?

Moses' concern with justice is seen in three episodes: an Egyptian mistreats a Hebrew (2:11); a Hebrew fights another Hebrew (2:13); and Midianites mistreat other Midianites (2:16, 17). His concern is for justice among all people, regardless of the identity of oppressor or oppressed. These chapters give examples of Hebrews doing wrong (2:13) and Egyptians doing good (2:5-9), as well as numerous examples of the opposite.

Dimension 3:
What Does the Bible Mean to Us?

What is the relationship between ignorance and fear? Between fear and foolishness? Between fear and violence?

Is it an exaggeration to say that the oppression of the Israelites follows directly from Pharaoh's fear of them? Do you think his fear follows from his ignorance of a history both peoples had shared? He seems ready to believe that Israelite and Egyptian women are fundamentally different (1:19) in his acceptance of the midwives' excuse for not killing the male infants. Can you identify anyone today who believes there are innate differences between racial or ethnic groups, apart from cultural differences?

Biblical writers are not shy about ascribing certain actions to God. At the same time, they also allow much range for human activity. Many people today believe in fate or luck and would be uncomfortable talking about the providence of God. Using the story in Exodus 2:1-10 as an example, how would you and other members of your class ascribe responsibility for the outcome? How much was luck? How much was God's doing? How much was due to human activity?

"THOSE WHO DO NOT KNOW HISTORY ARE DESTINED TO REPEAT IT."

How far do you agree with this statement? Can you see any specific examples of it in your own family? in the life of your local church? in the nation's life?

If you think there is some truth in it, what can or should we do about the appalling lack of knowledge of history among many of our own young people?

The action of Shiphrah and Puah, the midwives in 1:15-21, has been called "history's first recorded case of civil disobedience in defense of a moral cause" (from *Exploring Exodus: The Heritage of Biblical Israel,* by Nahum M. Sarna; Schocken Books, 1986; page 25). Under what circumstances is such civil disobedience justified?

Notice the wording of the two questions in the tinted area below. Do they ask the same thing with different vocabulary? Does even the choice of the words used for asking the questions seem to push for an expected answer in one direction or another?

> Many people today believe in fate or luck and would be uncomfortable talking about the providence of God.

Last Christmas I received a card in the mail. It said, "Holiday Greetings from all of us here at the Central Medical Clinic," and was signed by Dr. William Lyle, Dr. James Johnson, Betty, Lisa, Adele, and Constanza. I was irritated and showed it to several colleagues, friends, and students. The reactions were not split totally along gender lines, but nearly so. Women tended to understand, if not always to share, my irritation. Men tended to wonder why I was showing them an ordinary, mass-produced holiday card. Would you draw any connections between our contemporary use of names and titles and the way they are used in Exodus 1 and 2? Why do we know the names of the midwives, but know Pharaoh only by the title applied to all pharaohs?

Why are the "man from the house of Levi" and the "Levite woman" (2:1) identified by an extended family, but not called by name until later in the story (6:20)?

The discussion on page 6 notes that 2:12a does not say why Moses looked around before intervening in the beating of the Hebrew by the Egyptian. What was he looking for? for someone to help the Hebrew? for someone to back him up in his efforts to help the Hebrew? to see if anyone was watching him?

> • Do Christians have the right to "second guess" all authority?
> • Do Christians have an obligation to examine every law or command they are ordered to obey before carrying it out?

Choices between pure good and total evil are rarely difficult to make. But they are rarely made because few things in this world are so absolute. Our choices are nearly always between better and not-so-good, between varying shades of gray. For example, I do not know whether I am truly a pacifist, because I have never been put to the test. I would like to be one. When I have said this to people, I am sometimes asked the horrifying hypothetical question: "But if a madman had one of your daughters and was going to kill her and you had a gun, what would you do?" The answer, I think, is that I would shoot and try to kill the madman without harming my daughter. But the answer is also that I

think such an action would still be wrong. There may be times, in this fallen world, when our choices seem to be only between evil and more evil. Was this Moses' situation in Exodus 2:11-12? in 2:13? in 2:17?

Choices between pure good and total evil are rare.

Under what circumstances can violence be a legitimate Christian response to a situation? Or are there no such circumstances? We are those who follow the One who did not resist his own murder. Are we also forbidden all violence? What about spanking as a punishment for your child? What about hitting your spouse for forgetting an important appointment? What about various freedom fighters around the world? Does the nature of the oppression matter? For instance, does it make a difference if the oppressive regime they are opposing is a dictatorship? What if it is a situation of a racial or ethnic minority holding all power over a racial or ethnic majority as was the case for decades in South Africa? What about conflicts between people of the same race but different religious groups as in Northern Ireland?

Dimension 4:
A Daily Bible Journey Plan

Day 1: **Exodus 1–2**

Day 2: **Exodus 3**

Day 3: **Exodus 4–5**

Day 4: **Exodus 6–7**

Day 5: **Exodus 8**

Day 6: **Exodus 9**

Day 7: **Exodus 10–11**

GOD'S CALL—
INITIAL
REACTIONS

What to Watch For

Exodus 2 ended with God's hearing, seeing, looking upon, taking notice.
The plight of the Israelites will not be ignored. We will find that Exodus 3,
however, does not begin with God's working a spectacular miracle of
deliverance. God will appear to Moses, a man all alone watching a flock of
sheep. Be sure to read Exodus 3:1-17a, where Moses and God have a long
conversation at the burning bush. God commissions Moses as the one to
free the Israelites. Don't expect to find Moses at all enthusiastic. He will
finally agree to go back to Pharaoh's court with God's liberating message.
You will discover that liberation does not come immediately nor all at
once.

Follow the story in Exodus 4:30-31; 5:1-2, 10-13, 22-23.

Dimension 1:
What Does the Bible Say?

1. What do we learn about Moses and God in their conversation in Exodus
3:1-17 (and in all of Chapters 3 and 4)?

2. What makes Moses believe it is actually God speaking with him? (Exodus 3:1-6)

3. What do we learn about the elders and the Israelite people in their initial reaction to Moses' news? (Exodus 4:30-31)

4. How does Pharaoh react to Moses and Aaron? (Exodus 5:1-2, 10-13)

5. What has happened to the relationship between Moses and God by Exodus 5:22-23?

Dimension 2:
What Does the Bible Mean?

Exodus 2 ended with such a stirring note of God's activity that the beginning of Exodus 3 is quite different from what one might expect. Rather than a spectacular act of liberation by God, here is Moses out with his father-in-law's sheep. He is far from the action. He is so far away from "civilization" that he is said to be "beyond the wilderness." Perhaps that is an idiom for what we might term "in the sticks."

Moses is not entirely alone with the sheep. The One who is with him is called at times the angel of the LORD (3:2), or the LORD (3:4a), or God (3:4b). Moses' attention is caught by what is surely one of the best-known of biblical miracles: a bush that is on fire but does not burn up. He turns aside to see "this great sight" (3:3). God tells him to take off his shoes, because he is standing on "holy ground" (3:5). Note that the miracle of the bush is never mentioned again in the whole conversation. Having done its job by getting Moses' attention, it disappears into the background. The conversation between God and Moses is what is really significant.

In Exodus 3:6 God's self-identification is tied to history, to a specific history, which is called to mind by the names *Abraham, Isaac,* and *Jacob.* Naming the ancestors would also be a reminder of their relationship to God and the specific promises God had made to them (Genesis 12:2-3; 26:2-5;

13

28:13-15). They are all mentioned again at Exodus 3:15-16, 4:5, and 6:2, emphasizing continuity with the past while looking to the future. This also points up the contrast between God and the pharaoh, who was so unaware of his nation's history that he "did not know Joseph" (Exodus 1:8).

Exodus 3:7 repeats, in God's speech, three of the verbs of 2:24-25. (See page 7.) Earlier it was the narrator who used them. Now we know for sure that it is not just the narrator's imagination or wishful thinking. God admits to hearing, seeing, remembering.

Everything proceeds well until verse 10. "So come, I will send you to Pharaoh," says God. Moses' first response had been, "Here I am" (3:4). Now he replies, "Who am I that I should go to Pharaoh?" When Moses does get to Pharaoh's court and does deliver the message, Pharaoh's first response is a sort of grotesque echo: "Who is the LORD, that I should heed him?" (Exodus 5:2).

In 3:12 God answers, "I will be with you." This is the standard assurance to prophets and others whom God calls. Not, "Don't worry: everything will be just fine." Not, "It'll be easy." Not, "I promise nothing distressing will ever happen to you." Only, "I will be with you." (See, for example, Judges 6:16, Jeremiah 1:8.) Moses counters in 3:13 with several layers of "hypotheticals":

> "I will be with you." This is the standard assurance to prophets and others whom God calls. Not, "Don't worry: everything will be just fine." Not, "It'll be easy." Not, "I promise nothing distressing will ever happen to you." Only, "I will be with you."

If I go, and...

If I speak to the people, and...

If they ask your name, then...what should I say to them?

Moses is in no way committing himself to anything yet. What is he doing? Look at it logically. If the people already know God's proper name, why doesn't Moses? If, however, the people do not know God's proper name, then how will they know if Moses tells them the correct answer to their question about the name? No, something else is going on here.

In 3:14 God gives Moses an answer to his question, perhaps to Moses' surprise or even distress. The answer strikes us as puzzling, but a puzzling answer is an answer. God could perhaps have said, "How dare you ask such a thing!" or "You do not need to know that" or even "If I tried to tell you, you just would not understand." What is the answer God gives? The simplest English rendering is probably "I AM WHO I AM." That is not wrong, but neither is it right enough. Depending on which vowels one puts among the consonants, the first and last words of the three-word phrase might be translated "I am," "I will be," "I [will] cause to be," "I [will] become," "I [will] happen," and a few other options besides. The middle word is the all-purpose relative pronoun: "what," "who," "whom," or whatever the context requires. There is no rule saying the first word must

Icon of Moses from St. Catherine's Monastery located at the traditional site of Mount Sinai.

be translated precisely the same as the third word. Putting all these options together, we could have "I am whatever I will be," "I cause to be what I will be," and on and on.

Three times the verb part of the name is given in the first person singular. In neither English nor Hebrew does "I" have a specific gender. Thus, "I AM WHO I AM"—or however you choose to translate the sentence— does not carry any idea of either maleness or femaleness. If gender were of utmost importance in God's self-definition, then it would have been perfectly possible within the rules of biblical Hebrew for God to have said something like "I am he who. . . ." or "I am she who. . . ." Leaving it ambiguous allows for many more possibilities, including the possibility that gender may be irrelevant to God.

Bible translators have established a "code" to show what is in the original text: When Hebrew has the job description "God," the English says "God." When Hebrew has the title "Lord," the English says "Lord." When Hebrew has God's sacred name "YHWH," the English says "LORD" (or in rare cases GOD) with small caps for the "ORD" (or "OD").

The meanings of the name are more than can be given in a single word or phrase. Also God's name is not to be misused or used thoughtlessly (Exodus 20:7). As a reminder of these two things, we will do what Hebrew does. We will use only the consonants "YHWH" for the sacred, four-letter, personal name of God. (The fancy name for this is *Tetragrammaton*, which just means "four letters.")

Throughout the conversation, each objection that Moses raises, God patiently answers. You need to know my name? All right. You want some visible, tangible "proof" to show the people? All right: here are a couple of signs to practice now and one more to do later in Egypt.

Moses says he is not much of a public speaker and has not gotten any better since speaking with God (4:10). Finally, all out of excuses, rational or otherwise, Moses gets to the bottom of it: "O my Lord, please send someone else" (4:13). And, graciously, God lets Aaron become both companion and speaker for Moses.

Moses and Aaron receive a positive response from the Israelite elders when they first relate God's message (4:29-31). And then they have their first audience with Pharaoh (5:1-5). This time the outcome is different. Pharaoh immediately decides the people do not have enough to do, that they need to be kept busy so as not to think up such nonsense as going into the wilderness for a religious festival. "Let heavier work be laid on them; then they will labor at it and pay no attention to deceptive words" (5:9). When the Israelites protest, Pharaoh is adamant: "You are shirkers, shirkers! That is why you say, 'Let us go and sacrifice to the LORD' " (5:17, from *The Torah, The Five Books of Moses: A new translation of The Holy Scriptures according to the traditional Hebrew text*; The Jewish

16

Mudbricks being made today using the same method as the Israelites used in Moses' day.

Publication Society of America; 1962; page 106; hereafter referred to as NJPS). The Hebrew overseers protest to Moses and Moses carries the complaint to the LORD: "O LORD, why have you mistreated this people?

Why did you ever send me? Since I first came to Pharaoh to speak in your name, he has mistreated this people, and you have done nothing at all to deliver your people" (5:22-23). It is important to note here that God in no way rebukes Moses for lack of faith, but rather gives him reassurance that God's will ultimately is going to be done.

Beginning in Exodus 6:2 Moses' call is repeated, along with a repetition of the promise that God will indeed deliver Israel from Egyptian slavery. Then comes another of the most poignant—and realistic —of the Bible's verses. "But [the Israelites] would not listen to Moses, because of their broken spirit and their cruel slavery" (6:9).

Dimension 3:
What Does the Bible Mean to Us?

Look back at the encounter between God and Moses in Exodus 3–4. Who is talking to Moses? Is it God, the LORD, the angel of the LORD? All of those are mentioned. Does that mean there were three conversation partners? No, it is an indication of the difficulty of expressing in ordinary human words an extraordinary experience.

The difficulty is not in the reality of the experience. For example, have you ever seen a beautiful sunset? Have you ever tried to describe a sunset to someone who was born blind? Could you do it? Could you even explain the difference between red and green to a sighted person who happened to be color blind? The difficulty would not be in the reality of your perceptions, the reality of your experience, or your ability to distinguish between reds and greens. Neither would the difficulty be in the intelligence of the blind person nor her nor his willingness to try to understand. But without some level of shared experience, words by themselves sometimes cannot bridge the gap of understanding between persons.

God allows great freedom for us to respond, or not to respond. The bush burned, but no angel reached out to drag Moses over to see it.

How does God get people's attention today? Elizabeth Barrett Browning clearly had Exodus 3 in mind when writing these lines.

> Earth's crammed with heaven,
> And every common bush afire with God;
> But only he who sees takes off his shoes—
> The rest sit round it and pluck blackberries.
> —Elizabeth Barrett Browning, *Aurora Leigh*, 1857;
> Book VII, lines 280–83.

Freedom Not to Be Free

If Exodus is about freedom, then Moses must have the freedom **not** to take up the task God gives him. The Israelites must be free to remain in bondage to Pharaoh if that is their choice. Service to God must be embraced freely or it is merely the trading of one slavery for another. Freedom cannot be forced on anyone who would rather not be free. Although the terminology of slavery or servitude is used in religious contexts (Paul calls himself a servant/slave of Christ, for instance at Romans 1:1 and Philippians 1:1 [NRSV reads "servant" with "slave" given in a footnote]), unless it is a freely chosen servitude, it is not worthy of our Lord.

People who are in the ordained ministry often use the vocabulary of receiving a "call" from God. Have you ever talked to someone about such a call? Do you think God calls people today? Do you think God calls people *only* for ordained ministry?

Another word for "call" is *vocation*. Do you think God calls people to particular vocations? Can people argue with God the way Moses did? Have you, perhaps, had such an experience?

> Service to God must be embraced freely or it is merely the trading of one slavery for another. Freedom cannot be forced on anyone who would rather not be free. Although the terminology of slavery or servitude is used in religious contexts, unless it is a freely chosen servitude, it is not worthy of our Lord.

Pretend you are an ordinary Egyptian worker when Moses and Aaron request that all the Israelites get time off to go have a religious festival in the wilderness. How do you think you might react if another group of people gets such a bonus? Is it fair? You work hard too. And who's going to do all their work while they are gone? After all, you and your neighbors are not the ones responsible for the oppression of the Hebrews.

When a group of people is discussing oppression or discrimination or hardship, it is not uncommon for someone to bring up the issue of fairness in this way. What are some possible Christian responses?

I can nearly always find someone who is richer than I am, who is more privileged than I am, who is more of an "oppressor" than I am. And yet, if I look at the whole world, I am among the very richest, the most privileged just by being a citizen of the United States of America.

How much of oppression is relative? Many people have said, when talking about growing up during the Great Depression, for example, "We were poor but we didn't know it." Similarly there were people who defended the system of slavery in this country by saying that the slaves themselves were satisfied, and knew of no other system in which they would have chosen to live.

Names and the Name

Names are as important in these chapters as they were in Exodus 1 and 2. But personal names and their appropriate use are not a simple matter, especially when God's personal name comes into the situation.

19

DON'T CALL HIM BILL

"There are times when I take no offense at being called by my first name. A group of guys attending a ballgame or jazz concert shouldn't have to 'Mr.' each other, even if they've just met. I am flattered by readers who address me as 'Dear Bill,' if they follow it up with something like 'I've been reading you so long, you seem like a member of the family. . . .'

"What makes me uncomfortable—and sometimes a little cranky—is the false intimacy calculated to deliver some advantage to the person pretending the intimacy: the waiter, the insurance agent or the used-car salesman who has never seen me before and wouldn't recognize me a month later. These are people trying to convert what is clearly a business relationship for them into ersatz personal relationship for me, on the assumption that I will find it harder to say no to a 'friend.' Want to bet?"

(From "My Not So Lightly Given Name," by William Raspberry; *The Washington Post*, November 29, 1993; page A-19.)

Not only does God accept real give-and-take in conversation with Moses, God also seems willing to change plans in view of Moses' arguments. Do you think Aaron would have been recruited to speak for Moses, had Moses not raised so many objections? How does this match with your usual view of God? of prayer?

Dimension 4: A Daily Bible Journey Plan

Day 1: Exodus 12–13

Day 2: Exodus 14

Day 3: Exodus 15

Day 4: Exodus 16–17

Day 5: Exodus 18

Day 6: Exodus 19

Day 7: Exodus 20

Exodus
7:1-25
12:1-32

3

WORSE BEFORE BETTER

What to Watch For

The plagues begin at Exodus 7:10. The last of the plagues will be at 12:29-32. You may want to take the time to read the many surprising details reported in Exodus 7:14–12:32, some of which you will find charted in this study book, pages 23 and 24.

Do the plagues leave you with some potentially disturbing questions about God? God seems to be working both for and against the release of the Hebrew slaves. God seems at the very least to play favorites—and perhaps even to act with a disregard for the innocent bystanders. In the case of the "hardening" of Pharaoh's heart, it seems as if Pharaoh is being told by Moses and Aaron that God wants him to do one thing; then he is prevented by God from doing that very thing. In this portion of Exodus we will find the origins of the Passover, still observed in Judaism today (12:1-4, 21-28). In these chapters of Exodus (7–12) we will find a very realistic portrayal of human reactions to bondage, to hopes raised and then dashed, and to faith itself.

1. What happens when Moses and Aaron perform the first of the signs? (Exodus 7:10-13)

2. Why did Pharaoh not listen to Moses and Aaron even after the plagues began? (Exodus 7:20-24)

3. What preparations were the Israelites to make for the Passover? (Exodus 12:1-4, 21-22)

4. How is the remembrance of the Passover to be carried on? (Exodus 12:25-28)

With Exodus 7:8 the contest between the power of Pharaoh and the power of YHWH begins. Though it is a matter of grave seriousness, it is told with flashes of humor. Aaron throws down his rod, and it becomes a snake. Pharaoh's magicians throw down their rods and they too become snakes—but Aaron's rod/snake eats theirs! Picture the action as an animated cartoon! Humor is one of the hallmarks of the literature of oppressed peoples. It is apparent in some of the plague narratives. The frogs, for instance, are said to be in the Egyptians' beds, their ovens, their kneading bowls (Exodus 8:3).

There are other ways to "chart" the plagues that point up some interesting patterns. On page 24 are three ways to divide them, according to specific features. Notice the movement of the numbers.

What these charts show is that the first nine plagues are not nine random episodes, not nine natural disasters that "just happened." Even if any event itself is something that could occur as a random episode, the telling of the whole story is carefully crafted to make a point. There was an orderly plan behind it.

Comparing the Plagues and Signs

Plague/ Sign	Begins	Can magicians do?	Distinction	Pharaoh's first response
rod to snake	7:8	yes	Aaron's snake swallows magicians' snakes	heart is hardened
water to blood	7:17	yes		heart still hardened
frogs	8:1	yes		gives in momentarily
gnats	8:16	try but fail		heart remains hardened
flies	8:20		no flies in Israelites' camp	tries compromise
cattle are diseased	9:1		Israelite cattle unharmed	unchanged
boils	9:8	at home scratching		unchanged
hail/thunder	9:13		no hail on Israelites	"I have sinned"
locusts	10:4			tries compromise
darkness	10:21		no darkness on Israelites	offers compromise
death of firstborn	11:4		Israelites spared	releases Israelites

In the first of the series of plagues all the water in Egypt is turned to blood. Pharaoh's magicians can match this, so he remains unimpressed. Moses seems to be aware of the potential "natural" explanations to cloud the work of God. This may be why he makes Pharaoh set the time when Moses is to pray for God to remove the frogs (8:9-11). If the plague is removed at a time specified by Pharaoh himself, then he would have less basis for saying that the frogs would have gone away anyway, without Moses' intervention.

Other Ways to Compare the Plagues

1. Location of Moses' or Aaron's speaking to Pharaoh before the start of a plague.

Conversation w/ Pharaoh outside	Conversation w/ Pharaoh in his palace	No conversation with Pharaoh
1	2	3
4	5	6
7	8	9

2. Whether Pharaoh is warned before the start of a plague.

Warned ahead of time		No warning
1	2	3
4	5	6
7	8	9

3. Whether Moses or Aaron is the agent of the start of the plague.

Aaron the agent		Moses the agent	
1	2	4	5
3		6	7
		8	9

With the plague of flies comes the initial notice of a distinction being made between Israelites and Egyptians, the former being spared this pestilence. Pharaoh's court magicians do not even show up after the sixth plague—they are at home, too busy scratching their own boils to make an appearance.

In Exodus 9:18-21 warning is given about the coming hailstorm, raising again the issue of "innocent bystanders." Those workers and animals belonging to people who believed what Moses said were brought into shelter and protected. Those who did not were left out in the fields and were injured. Were they worse sinners than others? Probably no worse than those on whom a tower in Siloam fell (Luke 13:4). While we may gloat over wicked old Pharaoh, it is hard to rejoice over the deaths of people who had no choice in the matter.

Hardening the Heart

In Exodus 4:21 we read the first instance of a theme that is pervasive and troubling throughout the plague narratives, that of God's "hardening" Pharaoh's heart. Two things need to be said at the outset:

1. It is a difficult issue that apparently has no simple solution.

2. It may be made even more difficult by our standard/traditional English translations of the Hebrew.

Even in English, though, a careful reading will show variations that need to be taken into account. Sometimes we read "The LORD hardened Pharaoh's heart" (Exodus 9:12; 10:1, 20, 27; 11:10; 14:8). Sometimes no agent is listed: "Pharaoh's heart was hardened" (Exodus 7:13, 14, 22; 8:19; 9:7, 35). Other times Pharaoh himself is the subject of the verb: "He hardened his heart" (Exodus 8:15; 8:32; 9:34).

Sometimes it may be a matter of the omission of middle terms. If God is ultimately in charge of everything, this line of reasoning goes, then you might just as well say that something happened because God made it happen.

> If God is ultimately in charge of everything, we might say that something happens because God made it happen.

English translations tend to use one verb, "harden," in all these places. Hebrew uses three different verb roots and three different "variations" with these roots. Using different roots and different variations may be a way of signaling different meanings, or at least different nuances.

Let us look at some of the differences. One of the verbs used in these passages, *chazaq*, means "be(come) strong; have courage" in one of its forms. The other form used in these chapters can be translated "make strong, strengthen; support." So one might say God gave Pharaoh strength and courage, but he did not use it. Even for an absolute monarch, it would have taken some fortitude to stand up to the displeasure—the snickers? the whisperings of mental unbalance? the plottings of a palace coup?—of his own officials. And then there would be the practical problems: who was going to replace all that labor, for example? No, it would have taken just as firm a heart for Pharaoh to release the Israelites as for him to keep them in captivity.

It is intriguing to note that Pharaoh and God are each said to be the source of the hardening ten times. For the first five plagues, God is not said to intervene in the process. That is, one really cannot see Pharaoh as "an innocent, blameless individual whose integrity is compromised, and finally subverted, by the intervention of Providence. He exhibits an obvious and willing predisposition to cruelty" (from *Exploring Exodus: The Heritage of Biblical Israel*; by Nahum M. Sarna; Schocken Books, 1986; page 64). The narrator may be saying that what God is doing is reinforcing Pharaoh's own will, making him more "pharaoh-ish," rather than overriding his own tendencies.

Preparing and Remembering

Pharaoh's stubbornness makes the tenth plague inevitable. This plague is going to be different from the first nine in many ways. Moses gives his people elaborate directions to carry out in order to prepare for the plague and for their liberation, which will come immediately afterward. Look especially at Exodus 12:1-4. This theme of planning ahead, of sharing, of having enough-and-not-too-much is an important one. It will be discussed in more detail in Chapter 5 of this study.

In Exodus 12:21-28 are two more major themes. Moses tells the people to put some of the lamb's blood on their doorposts and to be sure to stay inside all night. This is not because God could not tell their houses apart from the Egyptians' nor because the angel of death could kill them by accident if they ventured outside. Rather, the people are given something to do for their own deliverance. They are to show by particular actions that they are indeed part of the community and that they trust God's word as it has been given them by Moses. But they must choose, by acting or not acting, whether to be a part of this undertaking. If they choose to participate, the symbolic action is well within their power to perform.

> The people are given something to do for their own deliverance. They are to show by particular actions that they are indeed part of the community and that they trust God's word as it has been given them by Moses. But they must choose, by acting or not acting, whether to be a part of this undertaking.

The other major factor in the preparations is remembering. While they are still slaves in Egypt, the Israelites are to be looking ahead to celebrating their deliverance when they get to the Promised Land. Even in Egypt they are to be letting their children see everything that is going on. Children who see new things will ask questions. And this is how their religious education will begin. Moses says, "When they ask, answer."

Dimension 3:
What Does the Bible Mean to Us?

> What constitutes an act of God? Does it have to be something that is impossible by human understandings? Does it have to be something we would call a miracle? Is "God" reserved for the spectacular, or does God have a place in ordinary daily life?

Pharaoh's magicians are able to duplicate the first three of the signs (rod to snake; water to blood; frogs). They try to make gnats but cannot. As long as they could do the same things as Aaron and Moses, we are told that Pharaoh's heart remained hardened (7:22).

It is possible to give some rational, biologically plausible explanations for the plagues. One of the strange things in this sort of argument is that it seems to be trying to protect the specialness of the Bible and its historical accuracy by giving natural explanations for the events described. A question to be raised is whether an event must be either unexplainable or contradictory to our understandings of the natural world in order for us to say that God is in it.

What constitutes an act of God? Does it have to be something that is impossible by human understandings? Does it have to be something we would call a miracle? Is that the only way God works? If we do understand something, if we can explain it, does that mean God is not involved in it?

An even more important question is: How does one discern what is God's action and what is simply "the way things are"? One might say that Pharaoh's reaction to plagues 1 and 2 exemplify the attitude, "If I can do it too, it must not be from God!" Is "God" a word reserved for explaining the spectacular, or does God have a place in ordinary daily life?

What does this say about a world in which natural science has unlocked some of the mysteries formerly reserved for God's knowledge alone? Does the increase in human knowledge mean a decrease in God?

There is another side to explore in the magicians' ability to duplicate the first few signs. What exactly did they do? They seemed to be able to do the same things as Moses and Aaron. But what help was that? If they had really wanted to show some independent power, if they had really wanted to do some good, then instead of producing more blood in place of water or calling forth even more frogs, they should have turned the bloody Nile to drinkable water or cleared some of the frogs out of the Egyptians' houses.

Sometimes we seem to see God's action better after the fact. Looking back, pondering an event, we may say, "God did indeed have a hand in that."

How much of God is in the interpretation of an event and not in the bare event itself? Consider, for example, the California earthquake of January 17, 1994.

• It occurred at 4:30 A.M.	rather than 4:30 P.M.
• It occurred on a Monday,	but a holiday Monday.
• It did kill people;	a relatively small number.
• Not all the planned retro-fitting of expressways had been completed.	Some roadways and bridges that had not yet been worked on did collapse.
• It may have been along a previously unknown faultline,	but people do know of other faults in that area and yet they continue to build and to live there.
• Although California has some of the most stringent building codes in the country,	not everyone honors them rigorously.

Taking these factors, and others you might think of, into consideration, how much of the devastation and death resulting from an earthquake is God's responsibility and how much is people's? Or is that even the right way to frame the question?

In Exodus 10:7 the court officials try to get Pharaoh to see the light. "Do you not yet understand that Egypt is ruined?" Their assessment of how out of touch the king is with the situation calls to mind the statement of an unidentified United States Army major in Vietnam reported by the Associated Press in the New York *Times*: "It became necessary to destroy the town to save it" (from *The Oxford Dictionary of Modern Quotations*, Tony Augarde, editor; Oxford University Press, 1991; page 7).

Can you find current examples of leaders who might need their hearts strengthened? Do you see some whose hearts you think may have been hardened? What about ordinary people? If God does indeed strengthen or harden hearts, is it only the hearts of leaders?

Before the final plague, everyone in the community was given the chance to take part. That is, Moses did not go around and put blood on the doorposts of all the Israelites. Each household was responsible for taking care of that matter themselves and in relation to their near neighbors.

Thus, they all had to be responsible for themselves.

To Think About Before the Next Chapter

● What is fair? Is fairness the highest goal for the Christian?

● Through what seems unfair, might God be trying to strengthen you for some task?

At the same time, Moses did not tell them to do anything that would have been too difficult for every household to carry out. No one had to perform great feats of strength or agility, no horrendously expensive equipment was needed, no one had to solve difficult intellectual puzzles. There was, therefore, a balance between every community member's having a stake in the outcome, everyone's being responsible, and limiting salvation to a favored few who were strong enough or rich enough or talented enough to do what was required.

> *Day 1:* **Exodus 21**
>
> *Day 2:* **Exodus 22–23**
>
> *Day 3:* **Exodus 24**
>
> *Day 4:* **Exodus 25–26**
>
> *Day 5:* **Exodus 27**
>
> *Day 6:* **Exodus 28–29**
>
> *Day 7:* **Exodus 30**

Exodus
14:5-14,
21-28

4

*G*ET READY, GET SET, FREE!

What to Watch For

When Pharaoh and the Egyptians discover that the firstborn of every family is dead, they will be eager for the Israelites to leave. The Israelites are ready to make their escape. God, however, will not lead them by the more "obvious" route, lest in the face of battle they give up and go back to Egypt (Exodus 13:17). When Pharaoh and his officials realize that the Israelites really are gone, they will have a change of heart. Their army will set out in hot pursuit. The Israelites will see the army bearing down on them. In terror, they will cry out to God and to Moses. Moses will instruct them to calm down, to stand firm, and to watch God's salvation (14:14). Moses will stretch his hand over the water and a dry path will appear for Israel. After all Israel has crossed and the pursuing army is in the seabed, the water will come back. And that will take care of the Egyptian army. God has promised deliverance, and Israel will be free.

Read the story for yourself in Exodus 14:5-14, 21-28.

Dimension 1:
What Does the Bible Say?

1. Why didn't the Israelites take the shortest route out of Egypt? (Exodus 13:17)

2. What happened when Pharaoh found out the Israelites were gone? (Exodus 14:5-6)

3. What happened when the Israelites saw the pursuing Egyptians? (Exodus 14:10-14)

4. What were Moses' instructions to the people? (Exodus 14:10-14)

5. What happened? (Exodus 14:21-28)

6. What was the response of the Israelite women? (15:20-21)

Dimension 2:
What Does the Bible Mean?

The map on the inside back cover shows the probable route taken by the Israelites in their escape from Egypt. Exodus 13:17 explains why they went this longer way around instead of going by the more direct route along the Mediterranean Sea. Think for a moment. If God is able to get them all out from slavery in Egypt, would it be impossible for God to get them safely past whatever forts and garrisons might be along that shorter route? Not likely. So why doesn't God lead them the shorter way? After all, it would probably even give more opportunities for God to work miracles on their behalf: smiting this group of soldiers, vaporizing those raiders. Exciting stuff!

But that is not how God works. God always shows divine concern for the freedom of the human beings involved. Because God respects human freedom, failure is one possibility in any undertaking. God knows the people well enough to know that if they had to face too many obstacles they might just turn around and head back to Egypt. Thus, God leads them by a route with less potential for difficulty.

Exodus 14:5-6 shows another aspect of reality. Once the crisis has passed and Pharaoh realizes that the Israelites are gone, he changes his mind again. This is the same pattern that we saw all the way through the plagues: while the distress or danger is present, Pharaoh will listen to God; when it is over, he goes back to his own preferences.

Because God respects human freedom, failure is one possibility in any undertaking.

The Egyptians are not the only ones who seem to be operating on short memories. The Israelites have seen God's working on their behalf several times already. Several plagues before the final sign on Passover night have made a distinction between Israelites and Egyptians (see the chart on page 23). The Israelites are described in Exodus 14:8 as "going out boldly." But in the face of a real and present danger—the fast-approaching Egyptian army—they quickly lose their boldness (Exodus 14:10).

In great fear, they turn on Moses. Suddenly everything is his fault. "We never wanted to be free," they now say. "We were perfectly happy serving as Pharaoh's slaves." But now, they accuse Moses, "you have taken us away to die in the wilderness" (Exodus 14:11). In some ways this complaint echoes their cries all the way back when they had to gather their own straw for brickmaking: "You have brought us into bad odor with Pharaoh and his officials, and have put a sword in their hand to kill us" (Exodus 5:21).

They are denying that they wanted to be free—which is understandable, perhaps, under the circumstances of their terror. They are saying that slavery in Egypt is better than death in the wilderness—which is understandable, certainly, when they believe they are facing immediate death. They see themselves trapped between the army and the water. Yet they are going farther. In both instances they are laying all the blame on Moses and none at all on Pharaoh and the Egyptians. If only Moses had left them alone; if only God had not offered to free them from bondage. Everything would have been all right without this "outside agitator" coming in, claiming to speak God's word, stirring up trouble.

Their reaction makes it look as if God were indeed prudent in Exodus 13:17—the longer route may well be the better one.

Moses does not scold the people for their fear. He does not try to defend himself, nor argue them out of their position. He says simply, "Do not be afraid." These soothing words are used several times in the Bible to people in similar situations. See, for example, Genesis 26:24, Deuteronomy 20:3-4, and Luke 2:10.

Then Moses gives them something to do. "Stand firm," he says, "and see the deliverance that the LORD will accomplish for you today" (Exodus 14:13). In many respects this is similar to the instructions about the Passover preparations:

The whole community is involved.
There is something for each person to do.
What is required is within the capabilities of each one.

They are given something to do to show their individual trust in God; they are given something to do as a community to show their unity with one another.

Note this also. The Israelites are told to stand firm. This is not a call to prepare themselves for battle. They are to be ready, not to fight, but ready to see the salvation God is going to work on their behalf. God will bring the salvation; they will not save themselves. Still, they are to be active participants, in that they have to "stand firm."

> The people are told to stand firm. This is not a call to prepare themselves for battle. They are to be ready, not to fight, but ready to see the salvation God is going to work on their behalf. God will bring the salvation; they will not save themselves. Still, they are to be active participants, in that they have to "stand firm."

Moses also tells his people to "keep still." This is a stillness of silence, not a command to be passive. Thus, it is not contradicted by the command to move forward, which follows immediately in Exodus 14:15.

On a careful reading, there seem to be some inconsistencies in the account of their crossing the sea. On the one hand, it is Moses' rod or hand that divides the sea (Exodus 14:16, 21, 26). On the other, it is the strong east wind that drives the waters back (Exodus 14:21). What happened to the Egyptians? Their chariots got stuck in the mud (Exodus 14:25), the LORD threw them into a panic (Exodus 14:24). The waters came back and overwhelmed the army so that they all drowned (Exodus 14:28), yet their bodies were strewn on the seashore (Exodus 14:30).

There are several reasons for these differences. In part, the differences occur because the record as we have it comes from several sources, no two of which report things from precisely the same viewpoint. In part the differences are here because, once again, the unique cannot be captured entirely in mere human words. Remember the beginning of the scene at the burning bush? We are told that God, the LORD, and the angel of the LORD appeared and called to Moses from the bush; yet Moses had one conversation partner and not three (Exodus 3:3-4). There is still another reason for the sort of composite picture we have in Exodus 14–15. We need to remember that we do not have a blueprint or recipe for salvation. There is no time when we can go out and do whatever needs to be done with no consultation with or aid from God.

> Be ready, not to fight, but ready to see the salvation God is going to work.

Even though people have tried to paint pictures and build models of the

Exodus event itself, and even though Cecil B. deMille used some clever camera work in the movie *The Ten Commandments*—upside-down waterfalls and all—the text is not clear precisely what happened when or exactly how God freed the Israelites and eliminated the threat of the Egyptian army.

"Trying to sort it out in a literal fashion, or suggesting that Israel considered the detail to correspond precisely to reality, is like retouching Renoir's paintings to make them look like photographs" (from *Exodus: Interpretation: A Bible Commentary for Teaching and Preaching*, by Terence E. Fretheim; John Knox Press, 1991; page 158).

God uses divine, human, and nonhuman agents: Moses and the wind are listed too. The eyes of faith will see God. But no one who chooses not to is required to acknowledge God. God seems to be willing to let us believe it was "only" a strong east wind that "just happened" to be blowing at the right time in the right place that allowed the Israelites to escape. The miracle was not carried out by, in Fretheim's phrase, "a divine snap of the finger" (*Exodus*, page 159).

> God alone is praised for gaining the victory, not Moses or the people. God has done for the people what they could not do for themselves.

The whole episode ends in celebration. Fear of Pharaoh and the Egyptian army has been changed to fear of the LORD. Crying out to the LORD and complaining to Moses has been changed to belief "in the LORD and in his servant Moses" (Exodus 14:31). Note carefully: it is God alone who is praised for gaining the victory, not Moses or the people. God has done for the people what they could not do for themselves. Their response is one of joyful abandon. They celebrate—singing and dancing and praising the LORD.

Dimension 3: What Does the Bible Mean to Us?

"Minds . . . Were Changed" (Exodus 14:5)

Sometimes the struggle is long; early victory is not the same as final victory. Human reality seems to be that big changes come slowly and with a sort of "two steps forward, one step backward, and another step sideways" pattern. This is true whether the topic is one individual trying to change a long-standing habit—giving up smoking, for example, or getting regular exercise—or an entire society facing changes.

Civil rights in this country could be used as an example. In 1954 the Supreme Court ruled that public schools could not require racial segregation. Forty years later we still have some segregated schools. Of course there are many reasons for that. In part it is because schools in an area reflect patterns of housing and employment, neither of which is entirely bias-free.

The February 1994 issue of *Circuit Rider*, the monthly United Methodist clergy magazine, used its front cover to highlight two articles: "A Black Pastor in a White Church: A Success Story," and "A White Pastor in a Black Church: What's His Advice?" If such "ethnic diversity" is news, that must mean that it is still a rare happening, even in the church.

Prudence or Foolishness?

If you were one of the Israelites in Exodus 14:10-14, would you have shouted at Moses that he was a fool? How do you decide what is prudent and what is foolish? The Egyptian army behind them was truly a threat to the Israelites; there was indeed water in front of them. Were they wrong to be afraid?

Perhaps the bigger issue is what they did in their fear. In both 5:20-21 and 14:11-12 they turn on Moses, rather than laying the blame for their plight on Pharaoh and the Egyptians.

All the way back in the story of the first humans, when God asked Adam what he had done, his response was, "The woman whom you gave to be with me, she gave me the fruit from the tree, and I ate" (Genesis 3:12). That is, he blamed his companion first and then God. The woman did not do much better, for her answer began by blaming the serpent (Genesis 3:13).

Can you think of other examples of such "scapegoating" today?

The community as a whole is told by Moses that they had to take part. And again, the required action was possible for everyone.

● Could God have saved the people without their faithful act?
● What does this say about how the church as the people of God should behave?

Who Makes the East Wind Blow?

As you read Exodus 14:21-28 think of a narrow escape you or a loved one has experienced. The proper relationship between signs and faith is an ongoing concern. It came up in the last chapter in terms of Pharaoh's court magicians and their ability to duplicate the first few signs Moses and Aaron performed. Here it is again.

We can look back on the Israelites and wonder how they could possibly have been scared, even with the Egyptian army coming. After all, they had seen so many things that God had already done on their behalf. If we had been there, we would not have been afraid. Or so we sometimes like to think.

Yet the "power" of a sign to engender lasting faith is weak. The danger of trying to rest our faith on signs is great. It might not be too much to ponder again Jesus' warning lest we be another "faithless generation" looking only for such signs. See Luke 11:29-32; Matthew 12:38-42; 16:1-4; and Mark 8:11-12.

God always leaves open the possibility that something was not a miracle; so that faith, if it comes, is truly free faith and not the result of coercion. God is not a spiritual or intellectual bully.

People, however, sometimes try to bully others into their way of thinking by pointing to signs of God's power. Interestingly, it is often negative signs people try to use on others. "Natural disasters" are said to be God's punishment. California and big cities seem to be frequent targets of this sort of thinking. Or disease is used as "proof" that the sufferer is a sinner. A male member of the clergy once gave a sermon to the effect that the increase in breast and uterine cancer among women in this country was God's punishment for women who were not content with their proper place in the home. The preacher was especially severe on women who were trying to "take over" the church from men.

To Think About Before the Next Chapter

• How do you know when you—either as an individual or as part of the church—should leave things as they are, rather than to try for something better?

• How do you—either as an individual or as part of the church—recognize God's signs?

36

Day 1: **Exodus 31**

Day 2: **Exodus 32–33**

Day 3: **Exodus 34**

Day 4: **Exodus 35–36**

Day 5: **Exodus 37–38**

Day 6: **Exodus 39**

Day 7: **Exodus 40**

5

*N*ow What?

What to Watch For

Israel's deliverance from Egypt will not be followed by immediate entry
into the Promised Land. Instead they will face the harsh circumstances of
the wilderness: lack of drinkable water (Exodus 15:22-25) and lack of food
(Exodus 16:11-21). To each difficulty God will provide a solution. The
solutions will involve the natural world and human effort too. Only after
each immediate problem has been solved will God add a law for the people
to follow (Exodus 15:22-26; 16:16, 19, 23, 29). That is, God will not use
the people's physical needs to "extort" their obedience. God's grace
always precedes God's law. God's law is one manifestation of God's
grace.

Read at least Exodus 15:22-25 and 16:11-30. To get the whole story,
read Exodus 15:22–16:36.

Dimension 1:
What Does the Bible Say?

1. What problem do the Israelites face at Marah? (Exodus 15:22-24)

2. How is the problem solved? (Exodus 15:25a)

3. What is the people's next complaint? (Exodus 16:2-3)

4. What is the LORD's response? (Exodus 16:11-21)

5. What is the relationship between manna and the sabbath? (Exodus 16:27-30)

Dimension 2:
What Does the Bible Mean?

After the miraculous escape from the Egyptians, after taking time for cele-bration and thanksgiving, the Israelites are now on their way to their new home. After three days they have not found any water. When they arrive at Marah they say, "Hooray! Water!" But it is brackish and unfit to drink. We read in a footnote that that is why the place was called Marah (meaning "bit-terness"). It is the same relationship between the name and characteristics of the thing named as calling Utah's Great Salt Lake the great "salt" lake.

"And the people complained against Moses, saying, 'What shall we drink?' " (Exodus 15:24). The people have been taken to task over the generations for this complaint, this "murmuring," as the King James Version puts it. But look at their situation. They have traveled for three days, undoubtedly using up whatever water supply they were able to carry out of Egypt with them. Now the water they have found they cannot drink. It seems almost worse than finding no water at all, to find water that turns out to be useless. They have a legitimate need. It is not just more com-plaining or pining for things the way they used to be back in the good ol' days. Compared to what they have said to Moses on other occasions (Exodus 5:21; 14:11-12), this is a mild reaction.

Moses cries out to God (using the same word used to describe the Israelites in Exodus 2:23). God shows him what to do to make the water drinkable. Then God says the Israelites were "put to the test" (15:25b).

"Murmuring" and "testing" are key elements in these chapters. We need, first of all, to be clear about what the terms mean. Part of that involves taking care not to assume that the way a word is used in one place must be exactly the same way it is used in every other place.

Most English Bibles use one of three words for the first term: "murmured" (KJV); "grumbled" (NJPS), (JB), (NAB); or "complained" (NRSV), (TEV), (NEB), (REB).

ENGLISH TRANSLATIONS AND THEIR INITIALS

KJV - King James Version
NJPS - *The Torah: The Five Books of Moses*
JB - *The Jerusalem Bible*
NAB - New American Bible
NRSV - New Revised Standard Version
TEV - *Today's English Version*
NEB - *New English Bible*
REB - Revised English Bible

In a number of incidents in Exodus 15–17 and Numbers 14, 16, and 17 complaining is reported. In some cases the people seem to exaggerate their complaint, as in Exodus 16:2-3. Still, to see here an actual rebellion against Moses and Aaron seems an overreaction on the interpreter's part.

The same pattern recurs throughout the whole series of stories now called "the murmuring tradition." God's calm reaction to the people is perhaps to show that God does not always "rise to the bait," that one does not automatically "push God's button" and get an angry response. God is able to look past the tone of voice, whining or fussing, and see the people's genuine need:

God cares.
God will provide.
God does provide.

There is no magic lightning flash that sweetens the water. Nor does God dispatch a little green alien to fix the brackishness. The solution comes in the form of an ordinary stick of wood, tossed into the water by the familiar figure of Moses. God uses elements of the created world and human helpers. We may also be meant to see a relationship between the first plague (changing water to blood) and this incident. Earlier the Egyptians "could not drink the water" (Exodus 7:24) because of what God had done. Now Israel "could not drink the water" (15:23), and God makes it drinkable.

"Testing" is never for its own sake alone, but for something more, something larger. It is used in conjunction with words of seeing, knowing, learning. The "test" is not to try to trick the people, not an attempt somehow to trip them up. Rather, the point is to see how well they will do, to show them, as well as to show the LORD, that they can and will follow.

Exodus 16:4 gives a certain discipline for Israel—so that "walking in God's law" (KJV) can become second nature; obedience can become a way of life.

To the complaint about their lack of food (Exodus 16:11-21) God has a different solution. Once again, in the way the story is told, the miraculous element is underplayed. And once again it seems that the people have a legitimate concern. If it is the "fifteenth day of the second month after they had departed from the land of Egypt" (Exodus 16:1), they have been on the way for about six weeks. They are hungry. In their hunger they remember how good most things were back in Egypt. What if they were slaves? Better to die quickly in slavery ("by the hand of the LORD," 16:3) than in freedom to die the slow death of starvation.

God gives Moses explicit directions to pass along to the people. There will be food ("bread from heaven," 16:4) each day. The people are to go out each day and gather that day's supplies. God says this is to see whether they will follow instructions. Day six will be different. They are to gather a two-day supply then, so as not to have to gather food on day seven, the sabbath.

That evening there is quail for supper. And in the morning there is "a fine flaky substance" all over the ground. The Israelites do not know what it is until Moses tells them, "It is the bread that the LORD has given you to eat" (16:15).

Moses tells the people to gather as much as they need and they do so. Then comes a surprise. Those who have worked energetically and gathered lots and lots turn out to have just enough. Those who have arthritic knees and three little children hanging onto their skirts cannot gather very much, but it turns out that they, too, have just enough.

Moses specifically warns them again not to try to save any for the next day. Some nevertheless try to hoard it, of course. And, in the wonderful phrasing of the King James Version, "It bred worms, and stank" (16:20).

The people need daily bread and weekly rest. God provides both.

On the morning of the sixth day they gather a two-day supply as they have been told. But on morning seven what happens? Sure enough, some people go out to gather manna. Moses is angry; the LORD wonders how long it will be before the people learn to trust, or at least to do as they are told.

Why are there these two rules: gather only one day's supply the first five days, then gather a two-day supply on the sixth day? It is not so much to show a miraculous property of God—that God could read a calendar. Rather it is to keep God linked to the everyday necessities of life in the people's minds. It is daily bread and weekly rest that the people need and God provides both.

Israel is supposed to live one day at a time, without hoarding against a day when God might just forget to send manna. They are not supposed to build larger and larger barns (Luke 12:15-21). There is even thought in the later tradition that the large and increasing gap between rich and poor is due to hoarding "manna" (Isaiah 5:8-9; Jeremiah 17:11; Amos 5:11-12; 1 Timothy 6:6-10). And Paul quotes Exodus 16:18 when exhorting the Corinthians to be generous in sharing (2 Corinthians 8:15).

The sabbath rules in conjunction with manna make two further points (Exodus 16:27-30). The sabbath is a time of rest for the whole community, built into the created order of things. And the rest is not to be at the expense of normal daily needs. Having been freed from oppression under Pharaoh, the people are not to trade this freedom for a new system of oppression called sabbath. Even aliens, strangers, and slaves are to be granted sabbath joy and rest (Exodus 20:10; 23:12; see also Matthew 12:1-13).

Dimension 3:
What Does the Bible Mean to Us?

Going to the Wilderness First

The excitement, the "on top of the world" feeling of a tremendous accomplishment is hard to sustain. When there has been a long buildup—to a wedding, a twenty-fifth anniversary party, a choir concert, a school play—there is nearly always a letdown immediately afterward.

Sometimes this sort of letdown, this disappointment, seems even worse when we have been expecting something good and have really been counting on it. Similarly, rationing their water use might have been easier for the Israelites to take if they had continued to find only dry ground than for them to have found water and then not be able to drink it.

People sometimes say, "I only expect the worst. If something good happens, I'm happily surprised. But if nothing good happens, I'm not disappointed." That is certainly an understandable position to take, especially if one has suffered many disappointments. Is it a mature Christian position?

One thing must be guarded against carefully: no one living in the Promised Land dare say, "The wilderness is not so bad; just trust in the Lord." That is a message that can come from someone out there with you in the distress, but not from one standing on the sidelines.

"Murmuring"

● Do you think the tradition is too hard on the Israelites to say they were complaining in Exodus 15:27-29? What should they have done?

● Are there times when it is better to put up with a bad situation rather than make a fuss about it?

POINTS TO NOTICE IN EXODUS 15:22-25

● The Israelites have a legitimate need.
● They take it to a leader (Moses).
● The leader/people consult God.
● God supplies a remedy:
—through the natural world
—with human cooperation

"Testing"

Testing is a normal and healthy part of growing up. Children test the limits parents set. Parents test the maturity of children by giving them more responsibility and seeing what they do with it. This growing and learning can include uncomfortable periods for both parents and children, but finally both generations manage to live through it.

Or again, one speaks of testing batteries to see if they still have any power in them. The point is to find the ones that actually work, not to see how many you can throw out.

HOW MUCH IS ENOUGH?

What do you think of Exodus 16:17-18?
● Is it fair that people who worked hard did not end up with more manna than everyone else?
● What is enough?
● Do these verses imply that having a savings account or a health insurance policy shows a lack of faith in God?
● What is the responsibility of community members to each other? After all, this text does not say that the swiftest manna-gatherers shared with the others. Is it up to God to even out any inequities that may exist?

Food and Faith

What is the proper relationship between food and faith? Note the order in which things happen. In both Exodus 15:24-25 and 16:12, 27-29, God first responds to the people's needs and then gives them a law or ordinance. The sequence is never reversed. God doesn't say, "First show me that you will obey, and then I will fix the water or send you food." Grace precedes law.

To Think About Before the Next Chapter

Consider all that God did for the Israelites before giving them rules and regulations. How do you see this relationship between law and grace in the life of your church? in your own life?

God is showing the people that there will be daily provision, but that it is not just built-in, not automatic, not mechanical. We cannot predict how God will act for our good, but are asked to listen to God and to follow God's initiatives.

Even if, as some have suggested, manna was a naturally occurring substance in that part of the world, God was still needed. The people saw the manna but did not recognize its significance and did not know what to do with it until they were told.

God's new creation is more than just spiritual—the "daily bread" to be prayed for includes daily physical sustenance.

The "What to Watch For" section on page 38 includes the statement "God will not use the people's physical needs to 'extort' their obedience." Is this too strongly worded? Perhaps we need to hear such strong language at times because the good news has become so familiar we do not really hear it in all its radicalness.

God's Grace Precedes God's Law.

God's grace does not come to us because we deserve it or because we are diligent about keeping the law. God's grace comes because God loves us.

> *Day 1:* **Leviticus 1–2**
> *Day 2:* **Leviticus 3**
> *Day 3:* **Leviticus 4–5**
> *Day 4:* **Leviticus 6–7**
> *Day 5:* **Leviticus 8–9**
> *Day 6:* **Leviticus 10**
> *Day 7:* **Leviticus 11–12**

$\mathcal{B}$EING CHANNELS OF BLESSING

What to Watch For

The Israelites will finally arrive at Mount Sinai. They will be there for the remainder of the Book of Exodus. Now God will speak to Moses and through him offer a covenant to the whole people. Reminding them of all that they have seen God do on their behalf (Exodus 19:4), God will propose that if they decide to obey God's "voice" and "covenant" they will become a "priestly kingdom" and a "holy nation" (19:5-6). When Moses reports this proposition, the people will agree unanimously (19:7-8a). Moses will duly report their decision to God (19:8b).

Watch for several crucial ideas not only for Israel, but also for the church as you read Exodus 19. These include *covenant*, being "a nation of priests," and being "holy."

Dimension 1:
What Does the Bible Say?

1. How does God communicate with the people at first? (Exodus 19:3)

thru moses — on the MOUNTAIN

2. What is the offer God extends? (Exodus 19:5-6)

treasured poss
priestly Kingdom
holy NATION

46

3. Whom does Moses tell? (Exodus 19:7)

elders

4. Who answers Moses, and what is the answer? (Exodus 19:8)

all—yes

Dimension 2:
What Does the Bible Mean?

This point needs to be made again and again: we must pay careful attention to the order in which things happen. Even when God is telling Moses what to say to the people God begins with a careful chronology: "You have seen what I have done on your behalf. Now, having seen that I do care for you and that I do keep my promises, I think we need to make a covenant with one another."

Another point needs also to be made repeatedly: God respects human freedom. God makes a genuine offer in verses 5 and 6. That is, there is no threat that "If you don't obey my voice and keep my covenant, I'll leave you out here to fend for yourselves." God does not say, "If you don't obey my voice and keep my covenant, I'll take you back to slavery in Egypt." God wants very much for the people to listen and to obey, but they are free to stop up their ears and to disobey. Later God will spell out negative consequences for disobedience, but that comes only after the people have agreed to be a party to the covenant.

This covenant that God is offering is not new. God and the people are not beginning a relationship that has no foundation in the past. The covenant was made with Abraham "and your offspring after you" (Genesis 17:7). Yet God does not bind forever those offspring without their own voluntary agreement. The Sinai covenant may be spelled out in particular terms, in more detail, than those that went before; but it is within the larger context of the covenant with Abraham, first articulated in Genesis 12.

Moses' role is special in that Moses goes up to talk with God. But Moses does not answer for the people. He is a messenger, an intermediary, and does not usurp the role of anyone within the community.

The details of God's offer are not spelled out at first. "If you will obey my voice and keep my covenant, you shall be my treasured possession out of all the peoples." Israel needs to recognize that God is not choosing them because there are no other options. God makes sure, going on to remind

St. Catherine's Monastery, built in the sixth century A.D., sits at the foot of Jebel Musa (Moses' Mountain), the traditional Mount Sinai.

them, "the whole earth is mine" (19:5). This should also remind them that they are not the only ones God cares about. God makes sure that everyone recognizes there are responsibilities attached if they do agree to enter into this covenant. The very next verse makes that clear: "You shall be for me a priestly kingdom and a holy nation."

This terminology of priesthood and holiness is both familiar and somewhat puzzling. The same terminology is used also in the New Testament, referring to the church as the people of God. "But you are a chosen race, a royal priesthood, a holy nation, God's own people" (1 Peter 2:9a). This New Testament usage continues the understanding that it is a calling, a specialness that is not simply for its own sake but that involves responsibility: "in order that you may proclaim the mighty acts of him who called you out of darkness into his marvelous light" (1 Peter 2:9b).

> God is not choosing the Israelites because there are no other options. God reminds them, "the whole earth is mine." This should remind them that they are not the only ones God cares about.

These three terms—special possession, kingdom of priests, holy nation—are intertwined. Israel is to be God's own people, set apart from other nations. This set-apartness, however, is not to be in opposition to other nations, but for their sake.

"Treasured possession" or "treasured people" is used here (and in Deuteronomy 7:6, 14:2, and 26:18) in relation to the covenant and combines the ideas of specialness and holiness.

To be "holy" is to be set apart, different, not ordinary. It is another dimension of specialness. The "Holy" Bible, for instance, is a book, but it is not just a book. (We will discuss in greater depth holiness and what it means to be a "holy people" or "holy nation" in Chapter 10 of this study.)

Up until this point the Israelites have seen what the LORD has done on their behalf. Most of the time they have been passive, mere onlookers. The participation has been primarily on God's side. But a relationship with God is not supposed to be a "spectator sport." Israel is being given the chance to become a more active participant. This is not to suggest that as the Israelites mature in their faith they will have less and less need for God. It is to suggest instead that the specifics of their relationship will change as they mature. Part of that changing relationship, part of that maturity, is the taking on of responsibilities, expressed in terms of being a "kingdom of priests" for the sake of the world.

The people answer Moses and the LORD with one voice. Did they answer too quickly, too easily? Perhaps. But God needs to know that they are at least willing to hear more about the covenant. Beginning in Exodus 20, the terms of the covenant will be spelled out. After hearing in more detail, the people will have another opportunity to decide if they want to be party to this relationship.

THE FUNCTION OF PRIESTS

Israel is to serve among the nations in a way similar to the function of priests within a nation. Thus, if they accept the covenant, all of Israel's life will be involved: life within the community, life with God, and life among all the nations of the world.

"Priest" is a troublesome term in some Protestant circles. It is viewed with suspicion by some. A "kingdom of priests" might not sound like a good thing to be. In neither Exodus 19:6 nor 1 Peter 2:9 does the idea mean that everyone is supposed to be ordained, nor that everyone has to be a religious leader. Rather, the nation as a whole, the entire faith community, is to represent the function of priesthood to and for the rest of the world.

What is that function? At its root, the nation is to be a channel of God's grace. This is not a new idea even in Exodus. At the first mention of God's covenant with a particular individual, in the call of Abram in Genesis 12, the notions of "privilege" and "responsibility" are paired. Abram the childless is promised descendants. Abram who is being called to leave his own land is promised a land. And Abram who is being offered these benefits of obeying God is told "in you all the families of the earth shall be blessed" (Genesis 12:3b).

Between the people's agreement and the actual giving of the detailed stipulations of the covenant is a period of preparation (19:10-15). They carefully stay clear of the mountain while they get ready for the solemn, formal agreement with God. They wash their clothes and abstain from sexual relations. The point is to make clear that, although God does indeed desire a close relationship with the people, God has to be treated in a special way. God is not just a bigger version of a human being. There is a poignant notice in Exodus 19:17: "Moses brought the people out of the camp to meet God."

There are signs in the natural world that something special is going on, with smoke and fire and the sound of trumpet blasts. Some translations, however, seem quick to translate everything into the natural realm. Verse 19 says, literally, God answered Moses "in a sound" or "in a voice." There is no Hebrew word there for "thunder." Maybe it sounded like thunder. Maybe it *was* thunder. We should take care not to over-interpret in the act of translating. Sometimes we cannot build a precise picture of what was going on. We would probably do well to admit that.

The point was made in "What to Watch For," on page 38, that God ~~~
Israel from Egypt before offering the covenant with its attendant rules and
regulations. Thus, one cannot say that God "extorted" the covenant.
People might agree to almost anything if they thought such agreement
would get them out of horrible slavery. God is careful also not to threaten
them with a return to slavery, or any other dire catastrophe, if they decide
not to accept the covenant.

But there is another side to it. If neither extortion nor threat, is it
bribery? Did God "play fair" by reminding them of what had already been
done on their behalf?

We can see glimpses of the problem in human relationships where there
is a great disparity of power. A private would only in the most extreme
instance ignore a general's wishes. The nurse follows the doctor's orders.
The student writes a paper to conform to the teacher's instructions more
than to express individual creativity. The cashier follows the routine prescribed by the storeowner. In such instances there is nothing wrong with
the "lower" person's following orders from the "higher."

But what about less formal, more personal relationships? Does the parent want the child to respond only out of fear of punishment or abandon-
ment? Does one spouse want the other to stifle his or her own individuality in order to do what he or she thinks (or guesses?) the spouse prefers? If
there is a great difference in power and freedom, it may be difficult for
each partner to have free choice.

God certainly has the power and the authority to be in the place of the
general, doctor, teacher, or storeowner in contrast to the private, nurse,
student, or cashier. But over and over again the Bible tells us that that is
not the sort of relationship God would prefer to have with us. Jesus uses a
well-known figure of speech, "Father." While this still has some cultural
overtones of "big boss," it is not as stark as "owner" would be.

Try to pretend to be God for a moment. How can you make an offer to a
group of human beings in a way that allows for their truly free response?
Is there any way at all that the huge, unbridgeable, power differential
between Almighty God and puny Israel can be overcome to allow for a
genuinely free choice?

Think again about the thunder and lightning and trumpet sounds in
verses 16, 18-19. The people have prepared for three whole days for this
meeting. Did God in some sense need to "put on a show" lest the people
be disappointed? Remember the story of Elisha and Naaman in 2 Kings 5?
Naaman went to Elisha to be cured of his leprosy. The prophet stayed

INSTANT RESPONSE

In Exodus 19:8 "The people all answered as one: 'Everything that the LORD has spoken we will do.'" Did the people answer too quickly, before they really knew what they were getting into? Might it have made more sense for them to have heard more of the details before committing themselves to this covenant with God?

In the Gospel of John, Jesus spells out some of what being his disciple means. After they hear some of the details, "many of his disciples turned back and no longer went about with him" (John 6:66).

inside his house and merely sent instructions for what to do. Naaman, who was an important man back home, was outraged and left saying, "I thought that for me he would surely come out, and stand and call on the name of the LORD his God, and would wave his hand over the spot, and cure the leprosy!" (2 Kings 5:11).

Might the people even have doubted it was God if there had not been something unusual they could witness? What does this say about our perception of God in the world?

God respects human freedom: Are there times when we would just as soon not have so much freedom?

Being Channels of Blessing

Being a "chosen race, a royal priesthood, a holy nation, God's own people" (1 Peter 2:9a) can make us feel pretty special. And it should. As God's children, we are special. But that "specialness" is not for its own sake. It is certainly not for us to feel puffed up and better than others. It is certainly not for us to feel that God cares more for us than for others of God's children.

Do people doubt God if there is not something unusual they can witness? What does this say about our perception of God in the world?

● What does the word *priest* mean for the average United Methodist? How would you explain *kingdom of priests* to the youth group in your church? Is your minister a "priest"?

● How would you explain being a "holy nation" to them?

Two parts of the covenant—land and family—are easier to accept than the third. The responsibility of being a channel of God's blessing may be harder. Can you think of ways your church is eager to receive blessings? In what ways does your church share blessings—especially to people outside the church?

Getting Ready

Do you have a special routine on Sundays? Maybe even a special Saturday night routine of baths and hair-washing and shoe-polishing? If so, why?

What do new clothes signify? What would you wear to meet with your child's teacher? to meet your bishop? to meet the President of the United States in the White House?

To Think About Before the Next Chapter

How can you, both as an individual and as a member of the church, live a life of "priesthood" and "holiness"?

Dimension 3: What Does the Bible Mean to Us?

Day 1: Leviticus 13

Day 2: Leviticus 14

Day 3: Leviticus 15–16

Day 4: Leviticus 17–18

Day 5: Leviticus 19

Day 6: Leviticus 20–21

Day 7: Leviticus 22

Exodus 20:1-19

7

PROMISES TO KEEP

What to Watch For

After the Israelites' extensive preparations, God will come to speak to them. They will be given an outline of the relationship they are being offered. This outline, this skeleton on which their relationship will be constructed, covers many topics in only *ten directives*. The first two of these commandments will discuss Israel's basic relationship to God. Three and four will deal with God-human relationship in the context of the community. The remaining commandments will have to do with more specifically human-human interactions, within the family group and within the whole human community. Still, these too will grow out of the underlying relationship between God and the created order, including the human world. Once they are examined in detail, the commandments will become harder to separate into discrete rules. They will appear to be an organic whole given ultimately for the health of the whole creation.

Read these commandments in Exodus 20:1-17.

Dimension 1:
What Does the Bible Say?

1. To whom are the words in Exodus 20:1-17 addressed?

2. On whom is the obligation to keep the commandments?

3. What areas of life are covered by these commandments?

Dimension 2: What Does the Bible Mean?

In English we use the same word *you* whether talking to one person or to six or to a thousand. In Hebrew there is one form for "you" if the addressee is singular and separate forms for the plural. Although God spoke to the assembled Israelites (Exodus 19:17) in a group, the commandments are stated in a singular form. It is as if God is saying, "Although you are a huge number of people, I wish to speak to each of you individually."

The number "ten" and the designation "commandment" are not used in this chapter. Instead, it begins, "Then God spoke all these words." Although ten is the conventional number, Jewish, Roman Catholic, and different Protestant traditions divide these instructions differently in order to come up with *ten*, the number that appears in Exodus 34:28, Deuteronomy 4:13, and 10:4.

1 God begins with self-identification. "I am the LORD your God, who brought you out of the land of Egypt, out of the house of slavery" (verse 2). This is the first commandment according to the Jewish numbering system. Unwritten but implicit the word *remember* seems to belong at the beginning. This verse, combined with verse 3, is considered the first commandment in Lutheran and Roman Catholic traditions. Then comes what other Christians consider the first command. "Do not go putting any other gods into my rightful place" is another way of saying "You shall have no other gods before me" (verse 3). Here as elsewhere, the Bible is much more concerned with practical than theoretical matters. Are there really other gods? Maybe. Maybe not. The important part of the message is, "Whether or not any other gods exist,

> Here as elsewhere, the Bible is much more concerned with practical than theoretical matters

you, my people, are not supposed to have anything to do with them. Do not waste time or energy arguing about the possible existence of alternative deities. The existence or nonexistence of other gods makes no difference. You are to worship this one God and no other. Period."

2 No images—because I am the LORD. ("You shall not make for yourself an idol, whether in the form of anything that is in heaven above, or that is on the earth beneath, or that is in the water under the earth," verse 4.)

"Jealous" (verse 5) is such a petty emotion, scarcely worthy of the LORD of all creation. Interestingly, the *Oxford American Dictionary* warns: "Do not confuse *jealous* with *zealous*" (Oxford University Press, 1980; page 356). That is precisely what has happened in the history of this verse, however. The Hebrew word is close to what in English we mean by zealous: fervently devoted; intensely earnest; actively enthusiastic. Indeed the Hebrew word is translated as "zeal" in many places, such as Isaiah 9:7 and 37:32.

> Translators . . . use different words so that the meanings stay the same.

English, being a living language, continues to change. Sometimes it takes Bible translators a while to catch up to such changes and to use different words so that the meanings stay the same. In this verse, the Jewish Publication Society's translation (NJPS) captures the flavor of the original by using "impassioned" rather than "jealous" to describe God. God cares. Idolatry matters, not because God is "jealous," but because God does not want the people to be living a lie, to be ordering their lives around a false idea, around a "god" that is not a god.

3 "Do not lift up the name of the LORD your God to emptiness or worthlessness or harm." ("You shall not make wrongful use of the name of the LORD your God," verse 7.)

In Chapter 1 of this study reference was made to the importance of names. This commandment is a warning not to treat God's name as if it does not mean much. Do not use it for frivolous purposes; do not use it in the service of falsehood. In most general terms the commandment means "Do not misuse the name of your God." It is also a warning not to think that by knowing God's personal name, you can control God, that you have power over God to get your own way.

4 "Remember the Sabbath to set it apart as special." ("Remember the sabbath day, and keep it holy," verse 8.)

God's blessing of a time for the cessation from regular labor is for the whole of creation. It is for the enjoyment *of* all the creation *by* all the creation. (In Deuteronomy 5:15 another reason for keeping the sabbath is given.)

5 "Honor your father and your mother," verse 12.

This commandment is likewise inclusive: both father and mother are to be "honored." Why? "So that your days may be long in the land."

The next three commandments are in the sparest possible language. In Hebrew there are only two words each: the negative particle and the verb.

WHO IS TO KEEP THE SABBATH?

You:	The person being spoken to, the individual hearing the words
Your son and your daughter:	All ages, all generations, are included
Your male servant and your female servant:	Both slave and free, both masculine and feminine
Your animals:	Both human and nonhuman creatures
The stranger/sojourner/alien within your gates:	Both natives and foreigners, even those with a different religion

6 "No murder." ("You shall not murder," verse 13.)
There is no single English word that will capture all the nuances of the Hebrew verb. The commandment does clearly say "No murder," meaning, in a general way, do not kill anyone on purpose. In other contexts it involves killing without the intent to kill—what we might term "manslaughter." Numbers 35 has detailed instructions for "cities of refuge" to which someone may flee for safety after killing someone by accident. It also details certain cases that are to be considered murder. The Hebrew verb in this commandment is used in both instances.

The commandment definitely outlaws murder. Whether it also forbids state execution, killing in warfare, or even the killing of animals for meat, cannot be decided conclusively on simple linguistic grounds. These are large and important issues. They are too important to have the decision resting on only one verse.

7 "No adultery." ("You shall not commit adultery," verse 14.)
In the most limited technical sense, adultery is a property crime committed by one man against another man by having sex with his wife. In a few instances women also commit adultery (see Ezekiel 16:38). In Jeremiah 3:9 the word becomes a metaphor for idolatry.

8 "No stealing." ("You shall not steal," verse 15.)
This prohibition seems simple to define, especially after the last two. It may be paraphrased, "Do not take by stealth or by violence something that does not belong to you."

9 "Do not answer concerning your neighbor a testimony of falsehood." ("You shall not bear false witness against your neighbor," verse 16.)

WHO IS COMMANDED TO HONOR PARENTS?

As nice as it is for girls and boys to treat their parents with respect, and use special holidays to show their love to Mother or Dad, "Honor your father and your mother" is a commandment given to adults. The words are not addressed to young children. The message reaches them when adult children treat *their* parents well. Then their own children will see and regard this behavior as an example. They in their turn will be cared for when they are old and infirm and perhaps an economic liability to the family.

One of the literal meanings of the verb translated "honor" sheds an interesting light on this commandment. In certain contexts the word means "make heavy." There may be a nuance here: to "heavy" one's parents is to continue to feed them, even when they are no longer economically productive for the family unit.

Even when they both are adults, children must honor their parents!

The wording of this commandment puts it in the public realm, even into a legal setting. But its wider meaning is surely not confined to matters of the courtroom.

10 "Do not covet anything at all that belongs to your neighbor." ("You shall not covet your neighbor's house; you shall not covet your neighbor's wife, or male or female slave, or ox, or donkey, or anything that belongs to your neighbor," verse 17.)

Wishing you had something *like* what your neighbor has is not coveting. Wishing that you had what *is* your neighbor's—and wishing your neighbor did not have it—is what the tenth commandment forbids. Not only wanting to have what your neighbor has but wanting to be just like your neighbor and do just what your neighbor does are all included here. By choosing to live in covenant with God, Israel is choosing to be different, to be a "priestly kingdom and a holy nation." God's people are not to be just like everyone else, in ancient days or today.

When God has finished reciting the commandments, the people are afraid. They back away from the mountain and plead with Moses not to make them hear God directly again. They beg Moses to talk with God and relay the messages to them. They promise that they will listen and pay attention. The LORD agrees to what we might call "Plan B." Abandoning "Plan A," direct communication with the entire community, God from now on speaks directly with Moses (accompanied sometimes by Aaron and the elders). He or they report to the rest of the Israelites.

What the people witnessed is described in a significant manner in verse 18. One way to translate the Hebrew, totally incomprehensible in English, is: "All the people saw the voice/sound . . ." ("All the people witnessed the thunder and lightning . . ." NRSV). By this use of words in an "impossible" way, the narrator is telling us once again that something happened that cannot easily be described. The people witnessed something. They saw lightning and smoke; they heard thunder. But there was something else here too. It was so different from their ordinary experiences that it has to be described as "seeing the voice."

Dimension 3:
What Does the Bible Mean to Us?

The Ten Commandments are not enough law for a human community. They must be interpreted and expanded for life within a community. An analogy may be drawn with the Constitution of the United States. The Constitution—even after adding the Bill of Rights (ten items) and additional amendments—is not enough to regulate the entire civil life of the nation. Both detailed law codes and developing case law are necessary to meet specific circumstances. But neither the law codes nor the case law can contradict the Constitution. When that happens, the newer rule is, by definition, "unconstitutional." All of the law codes in the Bible can, in one way or several, be traced back to the bedrock in Exodus 20 and its companion piece in Deuteronomy 5. What is unique about the Decalogue (Ten Words or Commandments) is that it is binding on every individual, whereas many other laws are specific to the particular circumstances. That is, every Israelite is required to refrain from idolatry, false swearing, murder, stealing, and all the rest. If one wants to be a member of this community, this is what one does and refrains from doing.

Much of the rest of the laws in the Bible function to make the "constitutional" law of the Decalogue case-specific. Because we are particular individuals living in particular times and particular places, we need the particularity of "case law" to help us live by the standards of the Ten Commandments.

Many of us are apt to break Commandment One, but rarely are we conscious of breaking it. Many of the things we are tempted to put in God's place are not evil in and of themselves. Patriotism, loyalty to one's employer, or professional ambition can all be positive. But they are also capable of taking over God's rightful place in our thinking.

Among the commandments are several that need special stress in our day. The misuse of God's name in Commandment Three is actually the misuse of God's power. It is asking God's power to call down curses. Is this, perhaps, what is done in using God as a threat, trying to scare children and others into proper behavior?

Commandment Five is often misunderstood. Israel did not know anything about Social Security or Medicare. If we as a society honor the elderly with these and similar programs, is the need for this commandment lessened?

Note that the wording is not "love" your parents. Love is an emotion and emotions cannot be commanded. Respect and honor—and continuing to feed!—are actions, and actions *can* be commanded.

Probably most of the jokes about the Ten Commandments center on Commandment Seven. For persons who are hungry, it is not sinful to want food. Hunger may lead us to sin if we steal the food, but hunger isn't sinful. Similarly, sexual

To Think About Before the Next Chapter
Look for an area in your life to which one of the Ten Commandments may speak a word of grace.

> "Who steals my purse steals trash;
>
>   . . .
>
> But he that filches from me my good name
> Robs me of that which not enriches him,
> And makes me poor indeed."
>
> —**William Shakespeare,**
> *Othello,* Act III, Scene 3

desire is not sinful. What we do with that natural instinct is what makes the difference.

Regarding Commandment Eight, it seems easy to understand that we are not to steal, rob, or shoplift. Are material goods the only things capable of being stolen? How does one guard against stealing someone's time? someone's reputation?

Dimension 4:
A Daily Bible Journey Plan

Day 1:	**Leviticus 23–24**
Day 2:	**Leviticus 25**
Day 3:	**Leviticus 26–27**
Day 4:	**Numbers 1**
Day 5:	**Numbers 2–3**
Day 6:	**Numbers 4–5**
Day 7:	**Numbers 6**

**Exodus
32:1-14
34:1-7**

8

. . . AND IF
THEY'RE
BROKEN?

What to Watch For

Moses will be on the mountain a long time and the people will be restless.
They will be wanting a visible symbol of the God who brought them from
Egypt. They will approach Aaron with the request that he make them
something to go in front of them. He will reluctantly gather their gold jewelry and fashion a calf. The people will be delighted: this is just what they
have been wanting. Aaron, however, will remain unsure. He will call for a
festival to the LORD. The people will celebrate enthusiastically.

Meanwhile, up on the mountain, the LORD will tell Moses he had better
hurry down because the people are out of control. God will threaten to
destroy them all and start anew with Moses. Moses will talk God out of
that plan, but when he arrives at camp (Exodus 32:19) he himself will be
so angry he will throw down and shatter the tablets of the law. Aaron will
give Moses an unbelievable alibi for his conduct while Moses was away
(Exodus 32:21-24). But God will have forgiven the people (Exodus 34:1)
and will instruct Moses to prepare two more stone tablets. In Exodus
34:6-7 the LORD will pronounce for Moses a fuller version of the divine
personal name.

Exodus 32:1-14 tells the story of the golden calf. Read also 32:15-24
and 30-35 to learn of Moses' reactions to the calf and 34:1-7 to discover
the account of the second giving of the tablets of stone.

1. Why are the people upset, and what do they want Aaron to do about it? (Exodus 32:1)

2. What does Aaron do, and why? With what results? (Exodus 32:2-4)

3. What is God's reaction? (Exodus 32:7-10)

4. What is Moses' reaction to God's plan? (Exodus 32:11-14)

5. What is Moses' reaction when he gets back to camp? (Exodus 32:15-20)

This is a straightforward story with clear lines between good guys and bad guys, between appropriate action and sin. Right? Actually, once one begins to look in detail, the clarity starts to blur, to fuzz around the edges—in a way similar to normal human reality.

Before we are too hard on Aaron for making the "golden calf," we would do well to look closely at the people's action. To say "the people gathered around Aaron, and said" is much too mild to describe what they do. The Hebrew says they "congregate against" Aaron. The atmosphere is probably closer to an angry mob at the town jail in an old-fashioned western movie than to a polite delegation of Girl Scouts asking permission to hold a picnic on the church grounds.

Aaron's response is also somewhat harsh. He tells the people to "tear off" their gold earrings to give him, all the people—wives, sons, and daughters. Did he hope they would be unwilling to part with their jewelry? Was he hoping thereby to put them off? Notice that "all the people" gave their gold earrings to Aaron. That is, it was not just a few malcontents; Aaron was greatly outnumbered.

Verse 4 is not clear about precisely how Aaron made the image; but it does use verbs of making, forming, and fashioning. (A quite different picture is given in Aaron's own description of his action when Moses questions him later. See 32:24.)

Verse 5 in Hebrew begins with a word that may be read in two entirely different ways, depending upon which vowels are inserted between the written consonants. The more traditional reading is "Aaron saw," though that does not fit smoothly with what follows. Another ancient tradition reads "Aaron was afraid. . . ." It is certainly plausible that, having seen and heard the people's reaction—"These are your gods, O Israel, who brought you up out of the land of Egypt!"—Aaron is desperate to get them back to the worship of the LORD alone. He was only trying to help, he was only doing what he thought was right, he was afraid for his own skin—whatever his reasons for doing what he did, he sees now that things have gotten out of hand. Quickly he builds an altar and calls for a feast to the LORD on the following day.

A religious festival sounds like a fine idea to everyone. They get up early the next morning to start the festivities, including offering sacrifices, eating, drinking, and playing. The last part of verse 6 is often translated in a way to suggest some sort of sexual orgy. The word, however, is "laugh" or "play" and is the root from which Isaac's name is taken. (See Genesis 17:19; 20:6.)

The scene shifts in verse 7 to the mountaintop where Moses is with God. God tells him he needs to hurry back down to the camp, because the people have run amok. Note the interesting use of personal pronouns. The LORD says neither "The people" nor "My people," but "Your people whom you brought up out of the land of Egypt." God then tells Moses what they have done. In general terms, "they have been quick to turn aside from the way that I commanded them." More specifically, "they have cast for themselves an image of a calf, and have worshiped it and sacrificed to it."

God then says because this is a "stiff-necked" people Moses should get out of the way so God's anger can get rid of them and a new start will be made with Moses. Moses talks God out of this idea. In the two columns in the box on page 65 you can follow the arguments each of them uses. Notice in particular the pronouns chosen.

64

God's arguments	Moses' arguments
32:7 **Your** people whom **you** brought up out of the land of Egypt.	32:11 **Your** people whom **you** brought out of the land of Egypt.
32:8 They have been quick to turn aside from the way that I commanded; made a calf; bowed to it; worshiped it; called it their god, the one who rescued them from Egypt.	32:12 Why let Egypt say: **you** brought them out for evil, to kill them? Have compassion on **your** people.
[That is, they didn't **remember** who I am and what I have done for them.]	32:13 **Remember** Abraham, Isaac, Jacob **your** servants to whom **you** swore:
32:9 I see they are stiff-necked.	"I will make **your** descendants as numerous as the stars.
32:10 I will make **you**, Moses, a great nation.	All the land I promised will be **yours** forever.

Verse 14 notes the LORD's "repentance" or change of mind about what the LORD had just said was going to happen to the people. It is as if God is willing to take them back. How are we to understand all this? Is God so fickle, so "jealous" (see Exodus 20:4-6), that at the first instance of a rival's showing up, God is willing to wipe out the whole nation and start over again with one man? Or might we look at this from another side? Perhaps this is a "testing" of Moses, as Abraham was "tested" in Genesis 22. Perhaps God wants to know just how faithful Moses will be in the long run. Perhaps God wants Moses to look at himself and discover just how faithful he will be. As far as the text is concerned, this incident remains between Moses and God. Moses is not depicted as going back to camp and saying, "Boy, you guys don't know how close you just came to being wiped out. But I saved you from God's wrath." The "lesson" of their conversation seems to have been for Moses more than for the people.

Moses is clearly on the side of the people while he is still up with God. But when he gets close enough to the camp to see for himself what they are doing, then his anger takes over. When he sees how the people have broken, at the very least, the first two commandments, he is furious. He throws down the tablets of the law, smashing the outward symbol of the inward reality they have already shattered.

Moses demands an explanation from Aaron, whom he had left in charge in his absence. Aaron does his best to explain away his participation. He had no choice, he says, and besides, when he threw the jewelry into the fire, "out came this calf!" What an amazing thing! Surely it cannot be seen as his fault.

God has Moses prepare another set of tablets for the laws to be recorded again. And then God pronounces the divine name once more. It is a fuller rendering this time, distilling into two verses the traits that have been exemplified in the episode of the golden calf. God does not reveal a name including "compassionate and gracious, slow to anger, abounding in steadfast love and faithfulness" until there has been an unequivocal demonstration that God does indeed have precisely those characteristics.

Dimension 3:
What Does the Bible Mean to Us?

Where would you put the blame for the "golden calf" episode? Can you make a case for the responsibility to be on Moses, Aaron, the people, and even on God?

1. Maybe Moses was having such a good time up on the mountain communing with God that he nearly forgot about all the people down in the camp. But then, wasn't this was a well-deserved respite for Moses from the rigors of leadership and the responsibilities of all those people?

Is it possible to be too involved with God? too involved with religion?

2. Perhaps Aaron simply had no backbone when it came to standing up to the people. He was second-in-command; they would have listened to him had he reminded them of the first two commandments. Or would they? The commandments might not have been in written form yet, but they had all heard the LORD speak them. Surely, if Aaron had just repeated them . . . or made everyone recite them in unison. . . .

3. Possibly God was right: the people are stiff-necked. They are never going to get the point or obey the law. Maybe it was all their fault.

4. Or perhaps God was lax. Perhaps God was having too good a time with Moses and not remembering the people down below any more than Moses was. Maybe it really was God's fault.

Why did the people want or need an image? Couldn't they still see the pillar of cloud during the day and the pillar of fire at night? Weren't they still finding manna outside the camp six days a week? Didn't the manna they gathered on the sixth day still last over to the seventh without spoiling? Why did they need something else, in addition to all those ongoing signs of God's continuing presence and care?

THE CALF: A VISIBLE SYMBOL

Is there anything comparable in your life to that visible symbol? I have a picture of my daughters on my desk at work and examples of their artwork on the walls. I like to be reminded of them throughout the day. But I do not need the reminder lest I forget what they look like; we all live in the same house. Because they are six and ten years old they still need Mom for lots of things. Yet I like to have visible reminders of them. Is this what the people of Israel wanted—just a familiar sort of visible reminder?

What is so wrong with a visible symbol? Do we need to do away with them all? even the cross? even the cross-and-flame logo of The United Methodist Church?

Belated Blessing

Where did a bunch of slaves get all that gold? Did they take it from the Egyptians when they escaped? (See Exodus 11:2-3; 12:35-36.) Might they have been better off in the long run had the gold not been available when they wanted Aaron to make them another god?

Why do you think Aaron called for a festival to the LORD? Was he scared when he saw and heard the people's reaction to the image? Was he hoping to call the people back to the worship of the only true God? Did he think that the calf would not be so bad if they also worshiped the LORD at the same time?

Think of other examples of calling on God at the last minute to "bless" something already established. When should we have been considering the LORD's will?

- Do invocations at the beginning of meetings become empty rituals that we continue without much thought?
- Does putting "In God We Trust" on our coins discharge our Christian responsibility for the way our money is used?

What did the people actually do in their festivities? The text is clear that they ate and drank. It also says they "played" (32:6). Play can be either good or bad; it is not necessarily sinful. Check the English translations among the other class participants. How many of these translations give a sinful, or sexual, connotation to this play? Might it say something about us if we are assuming some sort of sexual orgy?

67

Acceptance or Rejection

Once again we see a dramatic shift between what seems to be whole-hearted, enthusiastic acceptance of God's law and covenant and the whole-hearted, enthusiastic rejection of God. Quite often our lives seem to be like this.

• People who write out New Year's resolutions with great resolve on January 1 often find their zeal lagging long before January is over.

• People who experience a dramatic conversion are often disappointed, even crushed, to discover that their old besetting sins are still besetting them. Perhaps this is one meaning of the golden calf episode—to show us that not even meeting God at Mount Sinai changes people magically and makes them instantly faithful.

We need to remember the rest of the story too: in the face of this stubborn unfaithfulness, God continued to be faithful.

Moses was on the people's side in the argument with God until he saw for himself what was going on. Then he reacted with fury. Is this typical of human reaction? Things do not seem so bad when we hear someone else telling about them. When we are in the middle of the situation ourselves, however, do we lose perspective?

Do you think God may have been testing Moses with that offer to wipe out the people and start over again with him? Would that offer have tempted you? Can you fit this in, perhaps, with splits in churches or with differences that cause the formation of whole new denominations?

WHAT IS THE MOST SURPRISING PART OF THE STORY OF THE GOLDEN CALF?

• The people's demand for a visible god?
• Aaron's willingness to make something for them?
• The LORD's anger?
• Moses' talking God out of destroying the people?
• Moses' shattering the original tablets?
• Aaron's excuses?
• God's willingness to give the law again?

Day 1: **Numbers 7**

Day 2: **Numbers 8–9**

Day 3: **Numbers 10**

Day 4: **Numbers 11–12**

Day 5: **Numbers 13–14**

Day 6: **Numbers 15**

Day 7: **Numbers 16**

9

MORE THAN STERILE LEGALISM

What to Watch For

With Leviticus we will be in very different material from the sorts of things we have been reading up to this point. Instead of the familiar stories of Exodus we will have page after page of legislation. Many of these chapters will seem far-removed from our daily concerns. Who really cares about the intricacies of the sacrificial system? Yet Leviticus contains material with implications for today (for example, 2:4-13; 5:1-6, 11; 6:1-7).

Acknowledging the reality of sin, despite all their enthusiastic promises at Sinai, the Israelites will be like any other population. Leviticus will show concern that no one be left out from the remedy for sin. There is also the realization that sin has two dimensions: it disrupts the relationship between the individual and God and also the relationship between the individual and the neighbor. Leviticus addresses both of these concerns.

Read Leviticus 4:1-4, 13-15, 22-24, 27-29 to learn who is required to make sin offerings. Read the whole chapter to find out the specifics of the offerings.

1. Why are only portions of the offerings to be burned? (Leviticus 2:1-13)

2. What portions of the population have to make restitution for sin? (Leviticus 4:3-35)

3. Why are different people allowed to bring different sin offerings? (Leviticus 5:5-11)

4. What is required of a repentant thief? (Leviticus 6:1-7)

Dimension 2:
What Does the Bible Mean?

In the first lesson of this study it was mentioned that in the Hebrew tradition each book of the Pentateuch (the first five books) is called by the first (important) word of the book. Thus Exodus is known as *Shemot*, "Names." Leviticus is *Vayikra*, "And he called," taken from the first word of the book. The first two verses show that the people's request when they all were so afraid to hear God's voice is being honored by God. God summons Moses to the tent of meeting and tells him what to say to the people. Moses then relays the message. In this way, the people are not as terrified as they had been when they heard the sound of the Lord's voice themselves.

If the Ten Commandments function as a sort of "constitution" for Israel, more particular laws are still needed to cover specific circumstances. Leviticus gives us the details about much of the sacrificial system and the

71

reasoning behind parts of it. Because Israel did not make sharp divisions between the "religious" and the "secular" realms, laws concerning a wide variety of facets of life are included within Leviticus. Some of these are discussed in this and the next chapter of this book.

Some offerings are to be taken from the flocks and herds of the people. Others are produce, especially grain. Leviticus 2:4-13 details the procedure for certain baked offerings. As is the case with some of the others also (Leviticus 2:2b-3; 6:15-18, 26, 29; 7:6; and elsewhere), only a token portion is to be burned as a sacrifice or offering to God. The rest belongs to the priests and their families. In the division of the Promised Land among the tribes, the Levites are to be given no land. Instead, they are to preside over the sacrifices and live on offerings from the other tribes.

The Salt of the Earth

"You shall not omit from your grain offerings the salt of the covenant with your God; with all your offerings you shall offer salt" (Leviticus 2:13).

Several theories have been given for this requirement that sacrifices be sprinkled with salt. Perhaps it was originally to draw the remaining blood from the sacrificed animal (see Genesis 9:4). Perhaps salt was used in symbolic recognition of its preservative and antiseptic qualities. With the data currently available, we simply do not know why or how the practice began. But it did. And in this verse (and a few others) it is given as a perpetual commandment. The salt now functions as a sign of the ratification of the covenant between God and the people. The Israelites are enjoined specifically to remember the covenant with every single sacrifice. The sprinkling of salt on the offering serves as that reminder.

Remember what Jesus says to his disciples in the Sermon on the Mount: "You are the salt of the earth" (Matthew 5:13). Salt has many good qualities that it might be useful for the disciples to emulate for the sake of the world. It is a preservative and an antiseptic. It makes food taste good. As possible as all those are, Jesus may have had something else in mind too. He may also have been recalling this use in Leviticus and may have been saying to the disciples, "You are to be the sign of God's covenant with the whole world. You are to be a channel of God's blessing to the whole world." That is, there is a direct connection from Genesis 17 through Exodus 19 to Matthew 5, by way of Leviticus 2.

The first three chapters of Leviticus detail several types of offerings. Chapter 4 begins the discussion of sacrifices for sins, mentioning first inadvertent or accidental errors. Procedures are listed for the priests (4:3-12),

SALT AND THE COVENANT

"Then Abram fell on his face; and God said to him, 'As for me, this is my **covenant** with you: You shall be the ancestor of a multitude of nations' " (Genesis 17:3-4).

"Now therefore, if you obey my voice and keep my **covenant**, you shall be my treasured possession out of all the peoples. Indeed, the whole earth is mine, but you shall be for me a priestly kingdom and a holy nation" (Exodus 19:5-6).

"You shall not omit from your grain offerings the **salt of the covenant** with your God; with all your offerings you shall offer salt" (Leviticus 2:13).

"You are the **salt** of the earth" (Matthew 5:13).

for the people as a whole (4:13-21), for rulers (4:22-26), and for ordinary individuals (4:27-35). The general pattern is the same for all groups:
- one of the LORD's commands is broken;
- the infraction is brought to the attention of the offender;
- the offender takes the appropriate animal to the priest, laying hands

on the head of the sacrifice in symbolic transfer of the guilt to the animal.

Notice that no one is considered to be "above the law." Both rulers and ordinary people can commit sin. Religious leaders can sin. Even the community as a whole can be guilty of transgressing the LORD's instructions.

Sin is not always doing something wrong ("sins of commission"). One can also sin by failing or refusing to do that which is right ("sins of omission"). Leviticus 5:1 sounds hauntingly familiar. If you know something about a situation but keep quiet because you prefer not to get involved, that is considered sin.

Note the progression as laid out in 5:5-6:
- you realize that you have sinned;
- you confess the sin;
- only then do you bring the offering to the

priest for the ritual of atonement.

> Leviticus is clear that ritual does not replace an individual's penitence.

This sequence highlights some important things that have often been misunderstood by Christians in the past. First, while it is possible to sin by accident—to do something without realizing what you are doing—these are always infractions of previously known rules. No one is held responsible for what is not yet known.

Second, the atonement ritual does not precede the individual's confession of sin. Much less does the ritual take the place of such confession. Christians have sometimes criticized Judaism as a religion of "sterile legalism" or "empty ritual." The sacrificial system has been pointed to as one piece of evidence. That evidence does not hold up. Leviticus is clear that ritual does not replace an individual's penitence.

The ritual requirements are also sensitive to the varying conditions of the community members. Leviticus presents a "sliding scale" of offerings, depending on one's economic circumstances. The animal specified in verse 6 is a sheep or goat. Verse 7 specifies two turtledoves or two pigeons for individuals who cannot afford a sheep or goat. (You may want to look at Luke 2:24. Does this suggest anything about the economic status of Mary and Joseph?) Verse 11 covers those who cannot afford even the two birds, specifying instead a measure of flour. This progression shows two things: (1) a sensitivity to the inclusion of everyone, regardless of economic circumstances; and (2) the truth that atonement does not come only by the shedding of blood. No blood is involved in the offering of flour, and yet there is no indication given that people who make the flour offering instead of an animal sacrifice are any less forgiven than the others.

Exodus 20:15 gives the general commandment: No stealing. Leviticus 6:1-7 spells out a few of the particular circumstances covered by that general prohibition. These verses also make clear that such sins are committed against the neighbor who is deprived of property as well as against the LORD. Since both have been sinned against, both relationships must be restored. The relationship with God is restored by the guilt offering. The relationship with the defrauded neighbor is restored by returning not only the stolen or misappropriated property but by adding 20 percent to it.

Again the order is important. First, one is to make things right with the neighbor (6:4-5). Then one is to make things right with the LORD (6:6-7).

Once more the sins noted are both those of commission—robbery, for instance—and omission—finding lost property and lying about it instead of restoring it to its owner. "Finders keepers; losers weepers" does not have scriptural support!

Dimension 3:
What Does the Bible Mean to Us?

The introductory material to Leviticus in the *New Oxford Annotated Bible* says, "The nearness of God not only accentuates the people's sense of sin but prompts them to seek God in sacrificial services of worship. For . . . God has provided the means of grace whereby the people, forgiven and restored, may live in the presence of the holy God, avoiding those things that contaminate their health and well-being, and doing those things make them a holy people, separated for a divine service in the world (From "Leviticus," by Bernhard W. Anderson, in *The New Oxford Annotated Bible* [New Revised Standard Version], Bruce M. Metzger and Roland E. Murphy, editors; Oxford University Press, 1991; page 125 OT).

In a culture and religion where animal sacrifice is no longer practiced, can these early chapters in Leviticus have any meaning for us? Or are they of interest only to those who study the history of religious practices?

The question needs to be faced for Christians whether we still have that sense of the "nearness of God" that "prompts [us] to seek God in sacrificial services of worship." Or has our sense of God's nearness, especially as we experience it through Jesus Christ, prompted us in the other direction? Are we more likely to believe that "sacrificial services of worship" are less necessary for us rather than more necessary?

> We may have lost something important in assuming God has become our "pal." . . . It may be beneficial to our spiritual health to regain some sense of the awesome otherness of God.

This study in no way is advocating a reinstitution of animal sacrifice. The study does, however, raise the question of whether we may have lost something important in assuming God has become our "pal" in Christ Jesus. It may be beneficial to our spiritual health to regain some sense of the awesome otherness of God. God's presence is to be sought, but God's presence is also a fearsome thing, not to be toyed with.

- Leviticus 2:3, and other verses listed at the top of page 72, provide that only a portion of the people's offerings is to be burned on the altar. The rest is for the support of the priests and their families. How is this method of support similar to or different from the way your own pastor is supported? Some people believe that pastors should be "above" all discussion of finances. If they are truly answering a call from God, they should not be concerned about matters such as money. Others believe that, given the extensive educational requirements for their vocation, pastors should be paid more than they are now, that their salary should be comparable to someone in business with an equivalent education. Still other people believe that United Methodist ministers should be paid by the annual conference rather than by individual congregations. That way, the proponents tell us, income would truly be on a more equitable basis. That way, they suggest, it would be easier to match the "gifts and graces" of the pastor with the specific needs of the congregations. The economic level of the particular church would not be the final determination.

Which view or views do you think can be supported from Leviticus? Along with the economic needs of the priests, Leviticus shows concern he summer before I entered sixth grade our family moved from a middle-class neighborhood in one city to the inner-city of a different metropolitan area. We lived next door to the church where my father was minister. And I noticed, in a sixth-grader sort of way, that things that had not mattered in the old neighborhood took on different significance in the new.

Some neighborhood people did not feel comfortable coming to the Sunday morning worship service because their clothes were not the same as those of people who drove in from other areas. Some neighborhood people were embarrassed because they did not have enough money to put in the offering plate.

for the economic condition of individual worshipers. The varying requirements for the offerings indicates a variety of economic classes within the people of Israel.

How much of an economic mix is there in your particular congregation?

- Are most of the cars in the parking lot from the same price range? Do any look as if they are ten years old or more?
- Do most worshipers dress approximately the same way?
- Do most people live in the same, or similar, sorts of neighborhoods?
- What kind of reception do you think would be given to someone who appeared to be a great deal richer than the rest of your congregation? a great deal poorer?

Some problems related to our giving to the church could be overcome with the use of offering envelopes. But how might differences in dress be overcome? Private and parochial schools sometimes point to their policy of having children wear uniforms. When all students are dressed alike, nobody looks richer or poorer than anyone else. Does anyone dare suggest that worshipers wear uniforms to church on Sunday mornings? Is an equality of appearance the reason why the choir is usually robed? Should such things even matter to Christians? And if they should not matter but do, how can we move from one position to the other?

If Jesus' words to the disciples, "You are the salt of the earth" (Matthew 5:13), have to do with their being a sign of God's covenant to the whole world (Leviticus 2:13), how might that be lived out now?

Leviticus 5:11 specifies a measure of flour to be presented as a sin offering by someone too poor to afford birds or animals. Can this mean that there is more than one way for a person's relationship with God, which has been disrupted by sin, to be restored? Can the sacrifice of grain mean that blood is not absolutely necessary? Is God powerful enough and creative enough to effect atonement in more than one way? If it is indeed so, what might it say about our insistence that everyone worship as we do, believe as we do, act as we do, if they claim the name of Christian?

When all students are dressed alike, nobody looks richer or poorer than anyone else.

Dimension 4:
A Daily Bible Journey Plan

> *Day 1:* **Numbers 17–18**
> *Day 2:* **Numbers 19–20**
> *Day 3:* **Numbers 21**
> *Day 4:* **Numbers 22–23**
> *Day 5:* **Numbers 24**
> *Day 6:* **Numbers 25–26**
> *Day 7:* **Numbers 27**

NEIGHBORS AND STRANGERS

What to Watch For

Leviticus 19 will give us a constant refrain: the people are to be holy because their God is holy. God's people are to imitate God. Such imitation is to take very practical forms: provision for the poor to gather food; absence of hatred between persons; flagrant sin not being allowed to continue unchallenged. When we read Leviticus 25:1-28, 55, we will be reminded that even the animals and the land itself are to have a sabbath rest every seven years. Servitude and debts are not to last forever: every fiftieth year, property is to revert to the original families; people who were sold because of debt are to be released. Such actions will remind God's people that everything belongs to God and that they are servants of God. If God so cares for those who are servants, the people themselves should do no less.

Read Leviticus 19:1-2, 9-10, 17-18, 33-34 for specific ordinances given to the people by God. Read the rest of the chapter for additional background.

Dimension 1:
What Does the Bible Say?

1. What provision is made for the feeding of poor people?
(Leviticus 19:9-10)

2. How are individuals to treat one another? (Leviticus 19:17-18)

3. What is to be the relationship between native Israelites and foreigners? (Leviticus 19:33-34)

4. What is the sabbath for the land? (Leviticus 25:1-7)

Dimension 1:
What Does the Bible Say?

Leviticus 19 begins with a general framework for what is to come next. Following God's instruction, Moses is to say to all the people, "You shall be holy, for I the LORD your God, am holy." The foundation of the covenant relationship was spelled out in Exodus 19:6. Here in Leviticus we find its clear continuation in at least two directions.

1. The whole community is being addressed. This message is not for a spiritual elite or for the professionally religious alone. The covenant relationship is the basic identity for all members of the community. The objective is not to separate a few people to become saints, withdrawn from the world in contemplative or ascetic practices. Rather, the Torah's aim is to "create a holy people which displays its consecration to God's service in the normal day-to-day relations of farming, commerce, family living, and community affairs" (from "Leviticus," by Bernard J. Bamberger, in *The Torah: A Modern Commentary*, edited by W. Gunther Plaut; Union of American Hebrew Congregations, 1981; page 891).

"You shall be holy" is a message not for a spiritual elite or for the professionally religious alone. The covenant relationship is the basic identity for all members of the community.

2. While there is never any confusion that suggests the people of God are to become gods themselves, their action is based upon an imitative relationship. As God is holy, they are to be holy. (See Chapter 6 of this study for more discussion of holiness.)

79

In this chapter instructions are concluded over and over again with "I am the LORD" (19:12, 14, 16, 18, 28, 30, 32) or "I am the LORD your God" (19:3, 4, 10, 25, 31, 34).

One cannot legislate morality. Nor is it possible to command particular emotions. However, one can be warned of the corrosive effects of some emotions, especially if they are not handled responsibly.

Leviticus 19:9 and 10 instruct the people on how to gather their crops. Only the inner portions of fields are to be harvested; produce along the edges and in the corners is to be left for the poor. In the vineyards, no fallen grapes are to be harvested. They too are to be left for the poor. Coupled with "the poor" is "the alien." Both long-standing members of the community who are poor and strangers who have just arrived are to be allowed the gleanings of field and vineyard. No distinction is made between native and foreigner, between citizen and outsider. Nor is there any test for the "deserving" poor.

"Torah, unlike ordinary legal codes, is concerned not only with actions but also with attitudes. It recognizes how destructive bottled-up resentment can be and cautions us against wrong feelings as well as wrong acts" ("Leviticus," in *The Torah: A Modern Commentary*; page 896). It is true, of course, that one cannot legislate morality. Nor is it possible to command particular emotions. However, one can be warned of the corrosive effects of some emotions, especially if they are not handled responsibly. This is part of what Leviticus 19:17 and 18 do. They include a great deal of truth in compact form. In a more literal translation into English the words would be something like this:

> Do not hate your brother in your heart.
> Surely correct your kinsman;
> > And do not put sin upon him.
> Do not take vengeance,
> > Do not store up [wrath against] your people;
> Show love to your neighbor
> > [Who is] like you.
> I am the Lord.

We need to point out that the Hebrew language has not been required to undergo revision for the sake of inclusiveness. Even though the verbs in the above passage are all second person masculine singular, there is absolutely no indication that these verses mean to exclude women either as subjects or objects. That is, as a man is not to hate his brother, neither is a woman to hate her sister, a man his sister, a woman her brother, and so on.

There is a balancing between negative and positive verbs, a back and forth movement between things to avoid and things to be sure to do. "Do not hate" comes at the beginning; "[Do] show love" at the end. "[Do] correct" and "Do not take vengeance" appear in the middle.

Four different terms are used to describe those persons to whom one directs the prescribed actions. Each of them has the modifier *your*, which might be thought to limit them: your brother, your kinsman, your people, and your neighbor. Does it mean that anyone else's brother or neighbor does not count? Never! Not only do the teachings of Jesus counter this notion of limiting one's concern to one's own small group (see Luke 10:25-37), this chapter of Leviticus makes clear that the concept is a broad and inclusive one. (See the discussion of verses 33-34, page 82.)

> If you see someone sinning and simply ignore it, you are in effect putting sin—and its negative consequences—on that person.

In many English translations lines 2 and 3 differ from the translation written on page 80. The New Revised Standard Version, for instance, says, "you shall reprove your neighbor, or you will incur guilt yourself." This warning is clearly given at other places in the Bible, for instance, Ezekiel 33:6-8; here the Hebrew words say that if you see someone sinning and simply ignore it, you are in effect putting sin—and its negative consequences—on that person.

Next come two more prohibitions. The first verb is clear: "Do not take vengeance." The second verb by itself means "keep" or "store up" and needs some sort of object. What is to be kept or stored up? In the compact style of poetry, these two verbs may be meant to go together with the same object, as in "Do not take vengeance upon nor store up vengeance against" your people. The NRSV translation captures this well: "You shall not take vengeance or bear a grudge against any of your people."

Then comes the most familiar line of all. The traditional rendering is "You shall love your neighbor as yourself." The verse does not really mean "Love your neighbor *as much as* you love yourself" nor "Love your neighbor *the same way that* you love yourself." It is not a comparison of quantity or type of love. The comparison, rather, is between you and your neighbor; the statement being made is that you and your neighbor are the same. Not even gender separates one person or group from another, in spite of the title of a recent

> You and your neighbor are the same. Not even gender separates one person or group from another. Despite all the outward differences, at root, at the core of things, people are people.

bestseller, *Men Are from Mars, Women Are from Venus* (by John Gray; HarperCollins, 1993). Leviticus 19:18 says, to the contrary, that despite all the outward differences and all the troubles different groups of people have getting along with one another, at root, at the core of things, people are people. People are not divided up into different species. Love and loyalty are to be shown to other people purely because other people are who they are.

Verses 33-34 keep these points from being ambiguous. Verse 33 teaches not to oppress the sojourner, or resident alien. Verse 34 draws the clearest, most obvious distinction: the difference between the resident alien and the native-born citizen. But then, contrary to all expectation, the teaching dissolves that distinction: "The alien who resides with you shall be to you as the citizen among you." It continues with the same wording found in verse 18: "You shall love the alien as yourself." In this case, a clear reason is given: "for you were aliens in the land of Egypt." That is, external conditions of slavery or freedom, citizenship or homelessness, are just that: external conditions. They do not take away the basic shared humanity of all persons. On the basis of that humanity God calls for the love and loyalty of the community to be shown to all people.

Both these sections end with the refrain: "I am the LORD," with verse 34 continuing, "your God." It is God, not just some altruistic, fleeting emotion, standing behind these commands.

SABBATICAL YEAR AND JUBILEE YEAR (LEVITICUS 25)

The sabbatical year, as its name suggests, comes every seven years. It is a "sabbath" for the land. There is to be no plowing, sowing, or reaping. The jubilee year comes after a "sabbath of sabbaths," after seven times seven, the fiftieth year. In that year, not only does the land rest, but all property reverts to the original owner, or to that person's descendants.

The Torah is teaching us that land cannot be sold in perpetuity. All that is actually being sold is the number of harvests from that land until the next jubilee year. Thus, the place in the cycle is to be calculated and is to determine the price. Leviticus 25:17 is clear: "You shall not cheat one another," using the same word for "cheat" as for "oppress" (19:33): "You shall not oppress the alien." Even those persons who may have had to sell themselves into slavery are to go free at the jubilee.

The land is not to be sold forever, no people are to be enslaved forever, because all belongs to God. Because God is eternal and humans are transient, all people are "aliens and tenants" (Leviticus 25:23).

What images does the word *holiness* conjure up in your mind? Do you think of "holy people" as different from "regular" people? (Chapter 6 of this study discussed holiness in more detail. This might be an appropriate place to discuss any questions not adequately dealt with there.)

Most human languages use metaphors of the human body; no two languages divide the body in exactly the same way. When we speak of "sticking our neck out" we mean something quite different from "sticking our tongue out" or "sticking our nose in" someone else's business. We say we "love with our whole heart" although we also know that, biologically, the heart is a pump and does not really feel emotions.

Hebrew also has several figures of speech connected with body parts. "His nose burns" means he is angry. The "heart" for a biblical-Hebrew-speaker is where one thinks and decides and reasons, *not* where one feels emotions. Thus, to say "Do not hate your brother in your heart," means more along the lines of "Do not think evil or plot bad things against your brother," than "Do not have bad feelings about your brother."

> Keeping silent in the face of sin may allow the sin to continue. The sin may even be multiplied: on you for keeping silent; on the perpetrator if the sin continues; by victims if what is done to them leads them to other sin.

Keeping silent in the face of sin may allow the sin to continue. The sin may even be multiplied: on you for keeping silent; on the perpetrator if the sin continues; by victims if what is done to them leads them to other sin.

But saying "You shall reprove your neighbor" is easier than knowing just what to do in any particular instance.

Sometimes it is easier to speak to a stranger than to a family member or friend. Sometimes the most important things seem to be the most difficult to speak about to those we love. This seems to be the case regardless of whether the message is positive ("Thank you." "I appreciate what you did for me." "I love you.") or negative ("I think you may be drinking too much." "I'm uncomfortable that you seem to be lying to people so much.").

How does one approach a stranger with a reprimand? More than once I have been in a grocery store and seen parents (I assume) hitting or yelling at or otherwise mistreating children. It makes me sad. It makes me uncomfortable. But I have never been able to say to someone I have never met, "Please stop hitting that child."

It bothers me especially when my daughters are with me. Will they think what they are witnessing is just another acceptable way to treat children? They are old enough now that I think they know they will not be treated the same way. But I wonder if my silence says to them that I may love them but I do not care about any other children.

It is one thing to refrain from doing someone harm. It is something else to do someone positive good.

Does "do not hate" have exactly the same meaning as "show love"? Probably not. One reason many of these ordinances are put in both positive and negative forms is that they really do carry different nuances. It is one thing to refrain from doing someone harm. It is something else to do someone positive good.

How could we possibly have a sabbatical year for the whole society today? It is different now, isn't it? An industrial society cannot operate in the same way as an agricultural society.

Yes, that is true. But stop a moment: would it really be easier for an industrial society to take time off than for a subsistence agricultural economy—such as ancient Israel—to refrain from planting for a year?

What is the real purpose of the sabbatical year? Remember that these regulations are for the future, when the people who are presently out in the wilderness arrive in the Promised Land.

Remember also the kind of sabbath the people are experiencing while they are in the wilderness. On day six they find twice as much manna as on days one through five. And the extra manna on day six lasts for them to eat on day seven. Manna spoils when they attempt to keep it overnight on any other day.

If God can regulate the manna in that way, isn't it possible that God would regulate the crops in year six so that there would be enough to eat in a nonplanting year seven?

Maybe a better question to ask is back to the matter of purpose: allowing that God can do whatever God wants to do, why would there be a sabbatical year for the land?

Does anyone in your group have the sort of job that grants a sabbatical year? If so, maybe that person would be willing to tell about it: Who gets it? What happens during that year? What is the purpose of it? Do you see any connections between this and what is called for in Leviticus?

All is to be done in imitation of God: if God cares for the least, then we who consider ourselves God's people may do no less.

Are any of your members farmers or gardeners? Ask them to tell what they know about fallow ground or crop rotation. Are these in any way similar to the sabbatical year called for in Leviticus?

All is to be done in imitation of God: if God cares for the least, then we who consider ourselves God's people may do no less.

Love, as the word is used in the Bible, is an active word. It is action-oriented, not just an emotion. In many contexts it would be well to translate it "be loyal to." How can people today be loyal to neighbors? How can we be loyal to aliens? Or will such loyalty perhaps harm our loyalty to family members? (Remember the unnamed kinsman in Ruth 4:6?)

Dimension 4: A Daily Bible Journey Plan

Day 1: **Numbers 28–29**

Day 2: **Numbers 30**

Day 3: **Numbers 31**

Day 4: **Numbers 32**

Day 5: **Numbers 33–34**

Day 6: **Numbers 35–36**

Day 7: **Deuteronomy 1–2**

11

Is the Hand of the Lord Short?

What to Watch For

If you are familiar with various Old Testament prophets you may be aware that they often look back on the wilderness as a "honeymoon" in the relationship of God and Israel. We shall see that the actual stories have much unfaithfulness and complaining. The people will grumble about the food. Moses will complain about the burdens of his responsibility. His brother and sister will make a fuss about Moses' wife. Even the Lord will get angry. Still, the complaints will be answered, the hungry will be fed, the burdens of responsibility will be shared—even more than some people want at first. The people will come close enough to the Promised Land to send a contingent of spies to check it out (Numbers 13:1-2). The spies will return with a mixed message: most will be timid, afraid the inhabitants of the land will be too much for them. Only two, Caleb and Joshua (Numbers 13:30), will encourage the Israelites to trust in God and cross over into that land. But the people will balk. As a result God will tell them they will wander the wilderness until that generation has died out. Their children will enter the land they refused (Numbers 14:31).

Read Numbers 11:4-15 for the account of grumbling in the wilderness and 12:1–13:3 to find out about sibling jealousy and spies sent into the Promised Land.

1. What do the people want to eat instead of manna? (Numbers 11:4-6)

2. How does God propose to ease Moses' burdens? (Numbers 11:11-17)

3. What is Miriam and Aaron's main complaint against their brother? (Numbers 12:1-2)

4. What did the spies discover in the land of Canaan? (Numbers 13:26-28)

5. Why didn't that generation get to enter the Promised Land? (Numbers 14:26-32)

Names to Remember

The Cast of Characters found on pages 111–112 of this book will serve as a review of the study you are completing. Find another class member to help you. One should call out in random order the descriptions of the people listed. The other will try to give the name of the person described.

On another occasion the opposite approach might be used. Call out the names in random order, and ask your partner to tell something about that person.

In many ways these chapters sound like things we have heard before. The people complain about their food. Ever since Exodus 16:3 they have had similar complaints. They ask why they ever left Egypt. That has been a refrain from Exodus 14:11 on. (See also pages 39–42 of this book.) Moses complains about the people. He sets up a plan for the distribution of responsibility and authority. God even threatens to wipe out the Israelites and begin all over again with Moses. Moses argues the LORD out of that idea. (We have seen this sequence before, in Exodus 32–34, covered in Chapter 8.)

Numbers 11 weaves two of these stories together: the people's complaints about their boring diet of manna, and Moses' exasperation with all his responsibilities. Numbers 11:4 may be an attempt to soften the criticism of the people as a whole, for it blames the "rabble" among the people for raising the fuss about food. "If only we had meat to eat!" they grumble. "We remember the fish we used to eat in Egypt for nothing, the cucumbers, the melons, the leeks, the onions, and the garlic" (11:5). Interestingly, the items they remember do not include the meat they are crying for.

When Moses hears all the grumbling, he complains to the LORD. His first statements blame God rather than the faithlessness of the people. "Why have you treated your servant so badly? Why have I not found favor in your sight, that you lay the burden of all this people on me?" he asks (11:11).

THEY ARE TOO HEAVY FOR ME

Look carefully at the figures of speech Moses uses in verse 12. "Did I conceive all this people? Did I give birth to them, that you should say to me, 'Carry them in your bosom, as a nurse carries a sucking child?' " It is as if he is saying, "I'm not their mother. Why should I have to feed them?" But Moses continues as if his question is rhetorical. "Where am I to get enough meat to give to all this people? For they come weeping to me and say, 'Give us meat to eat!' I am not able to carry all this people alone, for they are too heavy for me" (verses 13-14). Moses seems increasingly distraught, ending finally with the plea (the bluff?): "If this is the way you are going to treat me, put me to death at once" (verse 15).

God's initial response is not to the complaint about manna. Indeed, it scarcely seems to be responding to Moses at all. In verse 17, however, God says that a portion of the spirit on Moses will be divided among the seventy leaders who are to come out to the tent of meeting.

Then God moves on to the issue of meat. Not only will the people have meat to eat; they will have so much of it they will get sick of the very sight of it. This meat will not be a one-day banquet but a whole month-long orgy. Now Moses does not believe his ears. "Where could you possibly get enough meat to feed this horde—and for a whole month?" God replies in a figure of speech, "Is the LORD's hand too short?" (NRSV footnote to verse 23). The hand or arm is often used as a symbol of power in biblical Hebrew. Thus the saying means "Is the LORD's power limited?"

Once again the focus shifts away from food to the sharing of power and authority. The seventy elders have gathered outside the camp. The LORD comes in the cloud and speaks to them. When a portion of the spirit from Moses rests on the elders, they prophesy. Then someone runs out from camp with the news, "Eldad and Medad are prophesying in the camp" (verse 22). Joshua is outraged. "My lord Moses, stop them!" he demands. But Moses deflects the anger. He is not trying for less of God's spirit among the people, but for more.

> Someone runs out from camp with the news, "Eldad and Medad are prophesying." Joshua is outraged. "My lord Moses, stop them!" Moses, however, is not trying for less of God's spirit, but for more.

One more shift of scene, and a shift of wind brings quail into the camp, knee-deep and then some, all around. As God had promised meat, they received meat.

Numbers 12 is a strange sort of story that, on one level, sounds like a typical family squabble. Moses had married a Cushite woman we are told, and Miriam and Aaron are "on his case" because of her (12:1-2). But at the end of their complaint comes the real issue: they are jealous. "Has the LORD spoken only through Moses? Has he not spoken through us also?"

God hears their fretting and calls them all out to the tent of meeting:

"When there are prophets among you,
    I the LORD make myself known to them in visions;
    I speak to them in dreams.
Not so with Moses;
    he is entrusted with all my house.
With him I speak face to face—clearly, not in riddles." (Numbers 12:8)

But, in the very act of speaking clearly to Aaron and Miriam, the Lord seems to be contradicting that assertion of speaking exclusively with Moses in that manner.

CATCHING QUAIL

In the Bible we are told how God provided meat for the Israelites during their years in the wilderness. Twice in the wanderings (Exodus 16:13; Numbers 11:31-32) we read that God sent flocks of quail for food.

These short-winged, sandy-colored birds found in Bible lands spend their summers in Europe, flying across the Mediterranean Sea to winter in Africa. That flight is long and tiring. When they stop to rest, quail stay close together on the ground and are so tired they are easily caught.

The quail covered the ground of the Hebrew camp, where they could be caught and sun-dried for preserving.

(From *Bible Info-Cards*, copyright © 1986 by Graded Press. Used by permission.)

When the cloud of God's presence leaves, they notice that Miriam's skin is diseased. (Many translations use the term *leprous*, but it is now known that what the Bible is talking about is not the same thing as Hansen's Disease, or what is now called leprosy.) Her affliction is interpreted as a sign of God's great displeasure, and Miriam must wait outside the camp the seven days of her punishment. All the people wait with her, not breaking camp until she is healed and can come inside the camp again.

The Israelites have now come close enough to their destination that God tells Moses to send spies to see what the land is like. Moses chooses a representative from each tribe and tells them to see what they can see and especially to check what sort of resistance they may meet from the current inhabitants of the land (13:17-20). After a forty-day excursion the men return. Their report is mixed. On the one hand they have found a land flowing with milk and honey and with spectacular produce (13:23, 27). On the other hand, they are afraid of the people, comparing themselves to "grasshoppers" in their presence (13:33).

The generation of complainers will not be allowed to enter the Promised Land, with two exceptions: Because Joshua and Caleb urged the people to trust in the LORD and to go up into the land, they will be permitted to enter the Promised Land.

Once more the Israelites complain, raising yet again their old cry, "Would that we had died in the land of Egypt!" (14:2). As they clamored for another god when Moses was delayed in returning from the top of Sinai, now some of them even suggest choosing another leader and returning to Egypt (14:4). Joshua and Caleb, two of the twelve spies, speak up. They list the splendid qualities of the land. They remind the congregation of God's promises. They urge the people not to rebel against the LORD. But the people will have none of it and threaten to kill them (14:10).

The Lord then comes and repeats the offer made to Moses in Exodus 32:7-10. "Enough of these complainers. They are never satisfied; they never believe in me and my care for them, despite all the evidence I have shown them. So, Moses, out of my way. Let me kill them off and then make a better nation beginning with you" (verses 11-12, paraphrased). As he did in the Exodus 32 conversation, Moses again argues God out of that idea. He does this in part by appealing to God's vanity, as he did before (Numbers 14:15-16). Moses also reminds God of the expanded name pronounced by the LORD in Exodus 34:6-7: "Forgive the iniquity of this people according to the greatness of your steadfast love, just as you have pardoned this people from Egypt even until now," he pleads (Numbers 14:19). God agrees, up to a point. The people are forgiven, but the generation of complainers will not be allowed to enter the Promised Land. Two exceptions are made. Because Joshua and Caleb urged the people to trust in the LORD and to go up into the land, they will be permitted to enter.

The next response of the people would almost be funny if it were not so sad. Having been told by Moses that God has taken their complaints and fears about Canaan seriously and has now forbidden them to go into the Promised Land, they decide that they *will* go in. Moses warns them not even to try. But they try anyway, and they are defeated.

Dimension 3: What Does the Bible Mean to Us?

Moses' misunderstanding about the Lord's ability to feed the people (Numbers 11:21-22) seems to echo in Jesus' disciples' several misunderstandings in feeding stories in the Gospels. Look at Mark 8:4, for instance, which is placed after the account of Jesus' feeding the five thousand (Mark 6:30-44). Or compare Matthew 15:33 with Matthew 14:15-21.

Do you think the Gospel writers might have had incidents such as Numbers 11 in mind as they collected and arranged their accounts of Jesus and the disciples? If so, what points might they have been trying to make? Part of the intention might have been not to compare Jesus with Moses or any other of the Old Testament prophets—remember that was who some people reportedly thought he was (Matthew 16:13-14)—but to equate the disciples with the Old Testament figures. Then, to continue the comparison, that would put Jesus in the Gospels in the same position as God in the story in Numbers.

Many of the incidents in Numbers 11–14 seem to be echoes of previous events and to resonate themselves in coming stories, not only of Old Testament events, but in the New Testament too. It may be that, despite their being clothed in very different garb from our ordinary lives, these stories point to some common features of the human race.

Moses seems to come to the end of his rope in Numbers 11:10-15. Other Old Testament characters also come to that point. They seem too burdened or too angry or too discouraged to go on.

● **Elijah**—"But [Elijah] himself went a day's journey into the wilderness, and came and sat down under a solitary broom tree. He asked that he might die: 'It is enough; now, O LORD, take away my life, for I am no better than my ancestors' " (1 Kings 19:4).

This speech comes after several adventures Elijah has in which God's care is manifested. After predicting a drought in the land, the LORD sends Elijah into the wilderness where he is fed by ravens (1 Kings 17:1-6). God provides food for Elijah, a widow, and her son, long after their supplies should have been used up (1 Kings 17:8-16). Elijah even prays successfully that God restore the life of the widow's son (1 Kings 17:17-24).

Elijah's greatest discouragement—the statement quoted on page 92, 1 Kings 19:4—follows his contest with the prophets of Baal on Mount Carmel, where he won a resounding victory (1 Kings 18:17-39).

● **Jonah**—"O LORD! Is not this what I said while I was still in my own country? That is why I fled to Tarshish at the beginning; for I knew that you are a gracious God and merciful, slow to anger, and abounding in steadfast love, and ready to relent from punishing. And now, O LORD, please take my life from me, for it is better for me to die than to live" (Jonah 4:2-3).

> Do you see any connection between God's replies to Moses, Elijah, Jonah, and Joshua and how God acts today?

Here too the discouragement seems to come at the conclusion of victory. By some measures, Jonah was the most successful prophet ever: he preached a minimal sermon and an entire nation repented. But it was not the response he wanted.

To what extent are these typical human responses to extreme situations? Do you see any connection between God's replies in these cases and how God acts today?

The Israelites as a whole even say something similar after hearing the report of the spies (Numbers 14:2-3). Do you think they are serious, or is it a bluff?

● **Joshua**—Joshua was outraged at Eldad and Medad. He thought they had no business prophesying at the "wrong" time in the "wrong" place—and they were the "wrong" people besides. They were not among those specifically chosen (Numbers 11:26-29). This story sounds very much like that of the disciples reporting that they had found someone healing in Jesus' name and had stopped him—because "he wasn't one of us." (See Mark 9:38-40 and Luke 9:49-50.)

These accounts also sound uncomfortably like what often happens in churches today. It appears sometimes that going through channels is more important than doing good; that making sure everything is done "decently and in order" (1 Corinthians 14:40) is more important than being open to the gifts of the Holy Spirit.

> It appears sometimes that going through channels is more important than doing good; that making sure everything is done "decently and in order" is more important than being open to the gifts of the Holy Spirit.

Or are we being too harsh? What has been the experience of your local congregation or of your Sunday school class?

Some congregations and individuals have been gravely harmed when people—supposedly acting on the authority of the Holy Spirit—stood up and made forceful pronouncements. Some people, for example, have claimed to be "told by the Lord" that it was an unforgivable sin for anyone to attend the church where a woman was pastor.

How do individuals, how do groups, balance the sometimes-competing claims of individual freedom in the Spirit and order for the good of the body? Take the issue of the ordination of women as an example. Not too long ago in nearly every Christian grouping the balance seemed at least "seventy at the tent" against it and only "Eldad and Medad" for it. Now many Protestant denominations recognize that God may call women to ordained ministry as well as to other manners of Christian life. Can one be a faithful Christian and be one of the two against the seventy? Can the faithful Christian position always be determined by taking a vote? Can it ever be determined in that way?

Dimension 4:
A Daily Bible Journey Plan

> *Day 1:* Deuteronomy 3–4
> *Day 2:* Deuteronomy 5
> *Day 3:* Deuteronomy 6–7
> *Day 4:* Deuteronomy 8–9
> *Day 5:* Deuteronomy 10
> *Day 6:* Deuteronomy 11–12
> *Day 7:* Deuteronomy 13–14

Deuteronomy 6:1-25

12

*I*SRAELITES— THE NEXT GENERATION

What to Watch For

We will find the Book of Deuteronomy presented as Moses' "farewell addresses." The people of Israel will soon cross over into the Promised Land. The congregation is made up of the now-grown children of the folks we left to die in the wilderness in Numbers 14. Moses reviews the story of the past forty years. Of great importance is the repetition of the law and the current generation's acceptance of the covenant relationship with the LORD. Over and over the point is made that by keeping the law when they get into the land, by keeping their proper relationship with God, the people will be able to make a good life for themselves and their descendants.

In Deuteronomy 6 you will find the **Shema** (shuh-MAH), the words Jesus identified as the Great Commandment (Mark 12:29-30; Deuteronomy 6:4-5), and important directions for passing on the faith to future generations.

Dimension 1: What Does the Bible Say?

1. Why are the people supposed to keep God's laws? (Deuteronomy 6:1-3)

2. How are they to remember the main point of the law? (Deuteronomy 6:6-9)

3. What is the danger they will face as soon as they get to the Promised Land? (Deuteronomy 6:10-12)

4. How are children to be instructed? (Deuteronomy 6:7, 20-25)

Dimension 2: What Does the Bible Mean?

Moses is instructing the people on the eve of their arrival in the Promised Land. Though he has led the people all these years in the wilderness, he knows that he "shall not enter" the Promised Land. (See Deuteronomy 32:49-52; 34:4.) He reminds the people of the major events of the past forty years of their history. He tells the story again of God's giving the law at Mount Sinai. He recalls how God first spoke so that everyone could hear. Then, because his voice terrorized the Israelites, God agreed to talk to Moses and let Moses relay the messages.

> The law is presented not as a burden but as a gracious gift. Keeping God's law is not to be done just because God demands it. Rather, the people are to live by the law "so that it may go well with you" (Deuteronomy 6:3).

Once again the law is presented not as a burden but as a gracious gift. Keeping God's law is not to be done just because God demands it. Rather, the people are to live by the law "so that it may go well with you, and so that you may multiply greatly in a land flowing with milk and honey, as the LORD, the God of your ancestors, has promised you" (Deuteronomy 6:3).

Deuteronomy 6:5 is among the best known of all Bible verses. The NRSV translates it: "You shall love the LORD your God with all your heart, and with all your soul, and with all your might."

Accurate as this is in terms of being a word-for-word translation, these words are not adequate to convey all the verse means. We need to focus our attention on four of the words used: *love, heart, soul,* and *might.*

● **Love.** The simple word *love* has as many shades of meaning in biblical Hebrew as it does in English. Someone can say "I love my daughters," "I love books," and "I love broccoli" without fear of being seriously misunderstood, although those are three quite different uses of one word. As we use the word in English, *love* tends to be something that either happens or doesn't. A mother cannot command her daughters' love in the same way she may demand lights out at 9:00 P.M. She may force them to eat broccoli, but she is powerless to compel them to love it. Similarly, a child cannot make a parent love Barney the TV celebrity despite the child's affection for the stuffed dinosaur.

"You shall be loyal to the LORD your God . .

We find Jesus quoting Deuteronomy 6:5: "Love the Lord your God . . ." in giving the "first and greatest commandment" (Matthew 22:37; Mark 12:29-30; Luke 10:27). But, if love cannot be commanded, how can we obey that commandment? In addition to the ways English uses the word, Hebrew and surrounding cultures and languages gave a political dimension to the word *love,* using it to mean "loyalty." The way to say slaves must be loyal to their masters was to say they must love their masters. Defeated rulers pledged fidelity to their conquerors using the vocabulary of love. It is not very likely that many pleasant emotions were shared, but the vassals knew better than to sign up with another overlord.

Thus, our commandment could start in English: "You shall be loyal to the LORD your God . . ." because the word translated "love" also means "be loyal."

● **Heart.** This love/loyalty is to engage all our heart. Now, *heart* is the exactly correct translation for what appears in the Hebrew text. The trouble is that when we hear *heart* once again we think of different things from what was meant long ago by Hebrew-speaking people. Human cultures tend to divide the body figuratively, to use particular body parts in figures of speech to stand for particular actions or characteristics. We may say "she felt the long arm of the law"; "he had his nose out of joint"; "the students were a pain in the neck." We also speak of "loving with our whole heart," even though we know that the physical organ we call the heart pumps blood and has nothing to do with the emotions we feel.

So far, so good.

The tricky part is that no two cultures/languages use these body parts in exactly the same way. While we say we feel emotions in our heart, the Hebrews used *heart* to stand for the place of thought and will, of decision and conscience. (Emotions for the Hebrews were said to be felt in the kidneys and—in the case of compassion—in the womb!)

> "You shall be loyal to the LORD your God *in all your thoughts and decisions* . . ."

Our paraphrase can now be expanded: "You shall be loyal to the LORD your God in all your thoughts and decisions . . ."

● **Soul.** The next important word is *soul. Soul* is a fine Christian word with a long and honorable history; but the word used in Deuteronomy had a meaning long before Christianity. *Soul* (*nephesh* in Hebrew) has two parts: first, it is what makes people and animals alive, but different from living plants. Note the Genesis 1:24 reference to "creeping things." Even the creeping things God made have *nephesh*. Centipedes and worms have "souls" since they are alive and are different from plants.

The second part of nephesh is individuality. Your nephesh is not like anyone else's because you are a unique living being. (Here is where some of the similarity with Christian conceptions of "soul" come in.) Your nephesh makes you alive; your nephesh makes you you.

> "You shall be loyal to the LORD your God in all your thoughts and decisions, *with all your aliveness and individuality* . . ."

Our paraphrase now reads: "You shall be loyal to the LORD your God in all your thoughts and decisions, with all your aliveness and individuality . . ."

● **Might.** The last of our four words is equally tricky. A standard biblical-Hebrew dictionary translates it "muchness, force, abundance, exceedingly." What is being commanded, thus, is a complete loyalty to God: a loyalty of thought and action and decision making, a loyalty that will be individual and not just following some crowd, and a loyalty that may require hard work.

If you look up Jesus' words in Mark 12:29-30 or Luke 10:27, you may think he added something when he quoted the verse from Deuteronomy. Jesus' "expansion" was not in adding any different meaning, however; but by using both *heart* and *mind* he was explaining for the Greek-speaking culture what was meant by the Hebrew concept of *heart* alone.

> "You shall be loyal to the LORD your God in all your thoughts and decisions, with all your aliveness and individuality, *as abundantly and completely as is possible.*"

These words of Deuteronomy 6:5, and the ideas behind them, are so important that they are to be thought about at home and away from home, talked about with the children, tacked up on the doorposts so you see them every time you walk from room to room.

Then comes a serious warning. The people are just about to enter the land long promised to their ancestors. As the LORD promised it would be, they will find it to be a good land, a land—in the traditional words—"flowing with milk and honey." They will move into houses other people built, eat produce from gardens and vineyards other people planted and tended, use water from cisterns other people carved out. When that happens, when they have finally begun to realize the dream that sustained their ancestors for generations, they are not to forget God. They may not need God in the same way their parents needed to be freed from slavery in Egypt; they may not need God to guide them through the wilderness any longer when they have settled down in the land. But God still wants to be in relationship with them. And God will notice, and respond, if they abandon God or if they decide to try out worship of some of the gods of their new neighbors.

Finally, what of the future? How are things to be continued into the next generations? Moses will not always be there to remind them of their history or of what God has asked of them. Deuteronomy 6:20-25 contains a deceptively simple plan: when the children ask, tell them the story. And note two significant features of the plan. First, it is implied that children are to be included in the life of the community. Otherwise, how would they have anything to ask about? Second, the adults are to tell the story as their own story. That is, the wording is "**We** were Pharaoh's slaves . . . ," not "Your ancestors way back in the past were Pharaoh's slaves. . . ." What such a practice may lack in strict historical factuality, it more than makes up for in theological truth.

Dimension 3:
What Does the Bible Mean to Us?

A major part of this chapter has been taken up in translating four words from Deuteronomy 6:5. Does that suggest some troublesome consequences? Do you wonder if other words in our English Bibles may not mean exactly the same thing as the Hebrew words—or the Greek words, when we get to the New Testament?

Serious problems face a translator any time a document is translated from any one language into any other. There are a number of reasons for this.

● Seldom are there exact matches, one word for another, whenever an idea moves from one language into another.

● Connotations that sometimes come along with a word scarcely ever match from one language to another. Sometimes this can be emotional content; sometimes particular words can call up specific memories.

● Human languages do not sit still. Teenage slang is not the only part of language that changes; meanings of words in all living languages change. For example, without the assistance of a dictionary it would be hard for most people to read and understand an English Bible as printed in 1611, the year the King James Version was first published, to say nothing of the 1540 "Geneva" Bible that the King James Version updated.

99

> What does it mean to love God with your whole heart? Some people have great difficulty with this if they think that *love* must always include "thinking nice thoughts about" or "never being angry at." Does it help to think of "being loyal to" God even in times of disappointment or anger?

● Some languages have words for objects or concepts that simply do not exist in another language. For instance, remember the description of Miriam's skin as reported in Numbers 12:10? It is described as being "white as snow." Most everyone in the United States has either seen snow or seen pictures of it. Because snow is something we are familiar with, we understand what color is meant. What would the word mean in a remote village of central Africa?

Numbers 11:7 describes manna as being "like coriander seed, and its color was like the color of gum resin." Could you draw a picture of that and color it accurately? Probably very few people in your class are personally familiar with both coriander seed and gum resin.

How much does all this matter? Is it something for "Bible scholars" that ordinary people do not have to worry about? In terms of having an accurate physical description of manna, it probably is not of major importance to the daily life of the Christian. But in terms of having an adequate understanding of what Jesus termed the "first and greatest" commandment, it matters, and matters a great deal.

What does it mean to love God with your whole heart? How can you live that out in your daily life?

> "Jesus died to take away your **sins**, not your **mind**." Do you think it is possible to love/to be loyal to God with our minds? Have you ever known someone who seems to think that religion and serious thought are really two different parts of life?

Some people have great difficulty with this if they think that *love* must always include "thinking nice thoughts about" or "never being angry at." Does it help to think of being loyal to God even in times of disappointment or anger? Think of relationships to people close to you. Have you ever said something on the order of, "I love her, but I sure can't stand her today!"

What are some of the ways it might be possible to be loyal to God with your mind?

In some campus bookstores a poster with a traditional portrait of Jesus has this caption: "He died to take away your **sins**, not your **mind**."

Do you think it is possible, really truly possible, to love/to be loyal to God with our minds? Have you ever known someone who seems to think that religion and serious thought are really two different parts of life? Or that religious convictions can be true if and only if they can be demonstrated scientifically to be true?

ARE YOU A SELF-MADE PERSON?

All of us depend on other people and their labors to be able to do what we want to do. I turn on my radio in the morning before I am even out of bed. There's no way in the world I could build a radio. I drink coffee with breakfast, but could not grow my own coffee beans. I drive a car on roads paved, or at least graveled, by others. I work in a building other people constructed. I communicate with people via telephones, fax machines, and computer e-mail. I know how to use them all, but I do not understand them. I need to remember not only my dependence on God, but my interdependence with the rest of the human community.

What is your reaction to the expanded ideas of *soul*? Do you think it really is possible for people to be loyal to God when they seem to do it in different, even opposite, ways?

Finally, do you think that what is being commanded here needs to be hard work? Isn't it possible just to love God and not worry about all the rest?

Do you fear that someone else may get more than you have or that you may have to do more work than someone else? A part-time tax assessor has described a common reaction he runs into. The assessed person starts by saying, "Now I believe in paying my fair share . . ." and ends with the notion that "my fair share" is less than everyone else's. Moses is reminding the people that they will be reaping the benefits of the labor of other people. He warns them not to get cocky about that, nor to forget what God has done for them.

Have you ever run into a "self-made person"? Maybe you consider yourself to be one. It is certainly true that there are wide disparities in this country in terms of the resources individuals begin with or have access to throughout their lives. Some people do seem to have lots of things handed to them on a platter. God's people discovered centuries ago that God is the giver of all that makes our lives significant. The path we walk follows the footsteps of Moses.

Dimension 4:
A Daily Bible Journey Plan

> *Day 1:* **Deuteronomy 15–16**
>
> *Day 2:* **Deuteronomy 17**
>
> *Day 3:* **Deuteronomy 18–19**
>
> *Day 4:* **Deuteronomy 20**
>
> *Day 5:* **Deuteronomy 21–22**
>
> *Day 6:* **Deuteronomy 23**
>
> *Day 7:* **Deuteronomy 24–25**

THAT WAS THEN; THIS IS NOW

What to Watch For

Moses will finish his charge to the people with some liturgical instructions:
when they get to the Promised Land, when they reap the first harvest, they
are to present the first produce to God. Moses also will tell the Israelites
what they are to say: the words are to be a summary of their story, a summary of their identity as a people. Moses gives them a final admonition to
remember, and to keep, God's commandments. The Book of Deuteronomy
will end with Moses' death, after he has looked over into the Promised
Land. The people will be poised to enter. They will have almost arrived but
are not quite there. Doesn't that historic reality parallel the theological
reality of God's people from then until this very day? The community of
faith is on the way to God's realm, but we have not yet arrived. We may
even be close enough at times to peer over into the Promised Land, but we
recognize that it is not yet our permanent residence.

Read Deuteronomy 26:1-11; 30:11-20; and 34:1-12.

Dimension 1:
What Does the Bible Say?

1. What is the worshiper supposed to say when presenting the basket of
first fruits to the priest? (Deuteronomy 26:5-10)

103

2. What is the relationship between the people and God supposed to be like? (Deuteronomy 26:16-19)

3. Are God's requirements too difficult to be kept? (Deuteronomy 30:11-14)

4. What is the situation of the people at the close of the book? (Deuteronomy 34:1-8)

Dimension 2:
What Does the Bible Mean?

Deuteronomy 26:1-11 contains instructions for a worship service when the Israelites are settled in the Promised Land. It tells not only what the people are to do—take a basket of the first of the produce they harvest to present to the priest before the LORD—but also what they are to say. In the space of five verses major portions of their history are recited. Most significant, the events are recited in a way that includes each generation, on into the future.

One verse, Deuteronomy 26:5, is the Israelites' "ancient history." It relates in briefest form how the Israelites got to Egypt. The writer of this verse was able to be so brief in part because of the assumption that the people reciting these verses would also know the stories behind them. They surely had heard the stories in Genesis 37–50 that fill in many of the details.

Deuteronomy 26:5 also begins with a very great contrast. "A wandering Aramean was my ancestor . . . [and he] lived there as an alien. . . ." That was the past. The present speakers are no longer wandering, but settled; no longer sojourners in someone else's land, but landowners in the very land promised of old to their ancestors.

At verse 6 the story takes a breathtaking shift. Did you notice it? Verse 5 is written in the third person: "he," the ancestor. Verse 6 shifts to first person plural: "we." Now, in terms of actual history, this is clearly not true. The people reciting the story in their new home are certainly *not* the same ones

104

who was the Aramean?

who were oppressed in Egypt. How do we know this? Because, according to the Book of Deuteronomy itself, Moses is speaking to the next generation, after those freed from Egypt have died in the forty years of wandering in the wilderness. Yet Moses is instructing them to say, "When the Egyptians treated *us* harshly and afflicted *us* . . . *we* cried to the LORD . . . the LORD heard *our* voice and saw *our* affliction, *our* toil, and *our* oppression. The LORD brought *us* out of Egypt . . . (Deuteronomy 26:6-8a, italics added).

Is Moses telling them to lie? No. In this way of recounting their history, they are telling a truth that is deeper than fact. When repeating the story of their ancestors, when reciting what God did for those of previous generations, they are at the same time incorporating themselves into the story. The story of their ancestors is becoming their own story as they recite it.

> The Hebrews are telling a truth that is deeper than fact. When repeating the story of their ancestors, when reciting what God did for those of previous generations, they are at the same time incorporating themselves into the story. The story of their ancestors is becoming their own story as they recite it.

Built into the worship life of the people, built into the very words of their liturgy, is a means for remembering their history and in so doing, remembering their own identity. At the same time it is a way for them to remember who God is, especially who God is in relationship to them.

"Once you were not a people, but now you are God's people."

(1 Peter 2:10)

"With all your heart and with all your soul."

(Deuteronomy 26:16)

Remember the discussion in Chapter 12 of the words translated "heart" and "soul"? The same two words are used in these two verses that are used in Deuteronomy 6. Verses 17-19 are a repetition, a summary, of the underlying promises made between God and the people all the way back at Mount Sinai. The basic covenant promises are these: the LORD will be the people's God; the people will be the LORD's own treasured possession. That is, they are agreeing to live in a close and reciprocal relationship with one another.

Deuteronomy 30:11-20 sounds as if Moses is anticipating objections from the people and is answering them before they even raise them. It would certainly be in keeping with their previous behavior for the Israelites to complain, "This commandment is too hard; it is too far away. Who can possibly go up to heaven and bring it down to us? Who could ever make it all the way across the sea and come back and instruct us so that we may be obedient? Who could possibly live up to such a thing? It is for gods, not mere humans."

"No," says Moses. "What I am telling you is neither too difficult nor too remote. You have it all right here. And you have the ability to keep it if you so choose." Moses makes clear that obeying God is not a matter for the spiritual elite but for every member of the community.

> Life and the good are on one side; death and evil on the other. How do they choose? How do they live out their choice? By loving ("being loyal to") the LORD or by turning to other gods? Either they walk in the ways of God, or they go after other gods.

Then in one final grand summation, Moses lays out the options before them. Life and the good are on one side; death and evil on the other. How do they choose? How do they live out their choice? By loving (remember: "being loyal to") the LORD or by turning to other gods? The figure of speech is that of walking. Either they walk in the ways of God (verse 16), or they go after other gods (verse 17). That is, the "choice" is not merely a sort of intellectual assent. It is not enough for them to say the words; meaning the words they say will involve the way they live their entire lives.

The foundation of all other sin is idolatry. Idolatry is not limited to setting up statues and bowing down in front of them. Idolatry includes all actions that put something else in God's rightful place. According to Deuteronomy, that is the way of death. Choosing the LORD and the commandments of the LORD is the way that leads to life, for individuals and for their descendants (verse 19). The choice is put before the people. It is a free choice; the matter of choice is their responsibility.

In verse 20 Moses rounds out the promise. The land into which the people are about to cross is none other than the land that God promised generations ago to give to the descendants of Abraham, Isaac, and Jacob.

When we get to Deuteronomy 34:1-12, Moses' work is finished. He has concluded his speeches/sermons reminding the people of their heritage, of God's love, of God's commandments. Now he climbs Mount Nebo, from which the Lord shows him the whole of the Promised Land, although he himself will not be allowed to enter it.

Moses dies and is buried. Since it is noted that "no one knows his burial place to this day" (34:6b), the legend is that the LORD buried Moses. The Israelites gave Moses the appropriate mourning time.

The Book of Deuteronomy ends with summary praise of Moses, the likes of whom has never since been seen. This conclusion can be thought of as Moses' epitaph: since no one knows the location of his grave, it is written instead in a book.

This is the ending not only of the Book of Deuteronomy, but of the Torah, the Pentateuch, the first major division of the Bible. And how does it end? With most everything still up in the air! With practically nothing settled! The Israelites are almost in the Promised Land, but not quite. The LORD has promised to raise up another leader after Moses is

106

gone, but Joshua has not proved himself yet. God through Moses has set before the people the choice of life and death, but they have not yet chosen.

Is this any place for an ending? Why didn't the story continue a few more chapters? Why didn't the people at least get across the Jordan River and step onto the Promised Land? or even settle into their new homes? *Why did't God forgive moses?* *READ 34:10*

Dimension 3:
What Does the Bible Mean to Us?

The significance of the shift in Deuteronomy 26:5-6 between third-person reporting of what happened to someone else and first-person affirmation of what God has done for us, for me, is one of the high points of the Torah. Can you think of any similar wording in Christian worship? What about the hymn "Were You There When They Crucified My Lord?" (No. 288, *The United Methodist Hymnal*). In terms of history it is nonsense. Of course none of us could possibly have been present almost two thousand years ago when Jesus was crucified. Yet in terms of theology it is profound. If it is true that Jesus died not only for people alive in his generation but also for those who came afterward, then that includes us. And if it is true that by our sin in our relationships with God and with each other we continue to crucify Jesus, then the sense of the hymn becomes clearer. And profound. And "sometimes it causes me to tremble."

> None of us could possibly have been present almost two thousand years ago when Jesus was crucified. Yet if it is true that Jesus died not only for people alive in his generation but also for those who came afterward, then I *was* there when they crucified my Lord.

Maybe a prior issue needs to be raised: just where does "our" history begin? **My personal history** cannot begin with my birth, but has to include at least something about my parents, doesn't it?

Where should **American history** start? with the Declaration of Independence in 1776? with Columbus's 1492 voyage? with the tribal traditions of Native Americans who lived here long before Europeans "discovered" America? How much of this is "my" history?

What about **Christian history?** Does it begin in the stable in Bethlehem or with a cross on Calvary? Or does it have roots a good deal deeper than that? Was not that wandering Aramean our ancestor too?

United Methodist history may, perhaps, start with John and Charles Wesley. But since they were both Anglican priests, shouldn't it contain some Church of England history too? And then there's the Evangelical Association, the United Brethren in Christ, the Methodist Protestants, the Methodist Episcopal Church, South, and so forth. They cannot be left out.

Do you live in a part of the country where a newcomer is anyone whose family has not been in the community for at least three generations? Is there any way that such people can ever "belong"? What does belonging mean?

Deuteronomy 26 could be considered a sort of "confirmation" liturgy, a "renewal" liturgy. It is a

John Wesley

Charles Wesley

"I'VE SEEN THE PROMISED LAND"

Martin Luther King, Jr., in a sermon to sanitation workers in Memphis, Tennessee, on April 3, 1968—the night before he was assassinated—found words that echo Moses on Mount Nebo:

"[When] I got into Memphis . . . some began to say the threats, or talk about the threats that were out. What would happen to me from some of our sick white brothers?

"Well, I don't know what will happen now. We've got some difficult days ahead. But it doesn't matter with me now.

Because I've been to the mountaintop. And I don't mind. Like anybody, I would like to live a long life. Longevity has its place. But I'm not concerned about that now. I just want to do God's will. And He's allowed me to go up to the mountain. And I've looked over. And I've seen the promised land. I may not get there with you. But I want you to know tonight, that we, as a people will get to the promised land. And I'm happy, tonight. I'm not worried about anything. I'm not fearing any man. Mine eyes have seen the glory of the coming of the Lord."

(Quoted in *A Testament of Hope: The Essential Writings and Speeches of Martin Luther King, Jr.*, edited by James M. Washington; Harper & Row, 1986; page 286.)

- How are new Christians incorporated into the body of Christ?
- How are new members incorporated into your congregation? into your Sunday school class?
- How do you, as a newcomer, become a member of a group, so that you feel that you truly belong?

way of reminding the people who they are as a community and who they are in relationship to the gracious God who has brought them to the good land they inhabit.

In Deuteronomy 30:15, the choice put before the people is listed as "life and the good" on one side, contrasted with "death and adversity" on the other. Many English translations, however, render the first phrase "life and prosperity." Do they mean the same thing? What may it say about us that we think of "the good" in terms of "prosperity"?

Almost but not quite there! Deuteronomy ends with the dream almost fulfilled, the people almost at their goal.

Overall questions

Dimension 4: A Daily Bible Journey Plan

Day 1: **Deuteronomy 26**

Day 2: **Deuteronomy 27**

Day 3: **Deuteronomy 28**

Day 4: **Deuteronomy 29–30**

Day 5: **Deuteronomy 31**

Day 6: **Deuteronomy 32–33**

Day 7: **Deuteronomy 34**

CAST OF CHARACTERS

(Exodus, Leviticus, Numbers, Deuteronomy)

Aaron—(AIR-uhn) (first mentioned in Exodus 4:14; 24:14)
Moses' brother, a priest who along with Hur was given authority in Moses' absence

Abihu—(uh-BIGH-hyoo) (Exodus 6:23; 24:1)
One of the sons of Aaron, designated to accompany seventy elders to Sinai

Amram—(AM-ram) (Exodus 6:20)
Moses' father

Bezalel—(BEZ-uh-lel) (Exodus 35:30–36:2; 37:1)
Skilled builder of the Ark of the Covenant and (with Oholiab) of the tabernacle

Caleb—(KAY-luhb) (Numbers 13:30, 14:6)
One of twelve spies who entered Canaan to report to the Israelites about conditions there; he and Joshua alone brought back a favorable report

Eldad—(EL-dad) (Numbers 11:26-29)
An Israelite who responded to God's spirit, about whom (with Medad) Moses said, "Would that all the LORD's people were prophets."

Eleazer—(el-ee-AY-zuhr) (Exodus 6:23; 28:1)
One of Aaron's sons

Eliezer—(el-ee-EE-Zuhr) (Exodus 18:4)
Moses' second son

Gershom—(GUHR-shuhm) (Exodus 2:22)
Moses' first son; his name meant "I have been an alien in a foreign land."

Hur—(huhr) (Exodus 17:10, 12; 24:14)
An Israelite soldier who with Aaron was given the task of holding Moses' arms upright when he grew weary during battle; also with Aaron settled disputes in Moses' absence

Ithamar—(ITH-uh-mahr) (Exodus 28:1)
One of Aaron's sons

Jethro—(JETH-roh) (Exodus 3:1; 18:1)
See Reuel

Jochebed—(JOK-uh-bed) (Exodus 6:20)
Moses' mother

Joshua—(JOSH-yoo-uh) (Exodus 17:8)
Moses' assistant and successor as Israel's leader

111

Medad—(MEE-dad) (Numbers 11:26-29)
An Israelite who responded to God's spirit, about whom (with Eldad) Moses said, "Would that all the LORD's people were prophets."

Miriam—(MIHR-ee-uhm) (Exodus 15:20-21)
Moses' sister (referred to but not named in Exodus 2:4)

Moses—(MOH-zis) (Exodus 2:10; Deuteronomy 34:7-12)
The leader who brought the Israelites from slavery in Egypt to the borders of the promised land of Canaan

Nadab—(NAY-dab) (Exodus 24:1, 9; 28:1)
One of the sons of Aaron designated to accompany the seventy elders to Sinai

Oholiab—(oh-HOH-lee-ab) (Exodus 35:30—36:2)
The skilled builder who with Bezalel built the tabernacle

Pharaoh—(FAIR-oh)
Ruler of Egypt; not a name but a title

Pharaoh's daughter—(name unknown) (Exodus 2:5-10)
Adopted the infant Moses

Puah—(PYOO-uh) (Exodus 1:15)
Hebrew midwife who along with Shiphrah disobeyed Pharaoh's order to kill all male Hebrew babies

Reuel (also known as **Jethro**)—(ROO-uhl) (Exodus 2:16-18; 3:1; 18:1)
Moses' father-in-law; priest of Midian

Shiphrah—(SHIF -ruh) (Exodus 1:15)
Hebrew midwife who along with Puah disobeyed Pharaoh's order to kill all male Hebrew babies

Zipporah—(zi-POR-uh) (Exodus 2:21)
Moses' wife; daughter of the priest of Midian

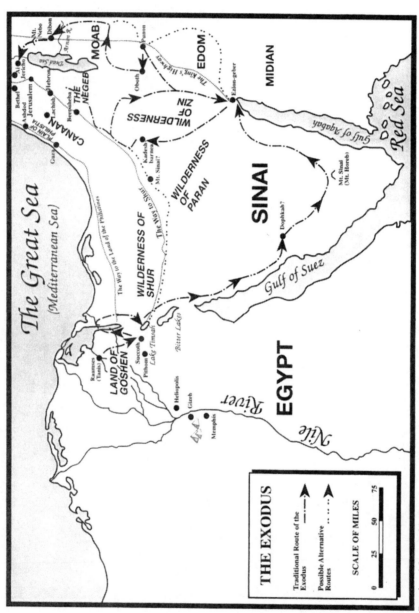

THE EXODUS

Traditional Route of the Exodus

Possible Alternative Routes

SCALE OF MILES

0   25   50   75